TABLE OF CONTENTS

BAKING BASICS 4

PREPARATION & SAFETY 6

INGREDIENTS 10

TECHNIQUES 16

CAKES & CUPCAKES 24
- Luscious Lemon Pound Cake 26
- Heavenly Angel Food Cake 28
- Tunnel of Fudge Cake 30
- Chocolate Flourless Cake 32
- Berry Shortcake 34
- Honey Nut Cake 36
- Festive Apple Kuchen 38
- Velvety Chocolate Cake 40
- Tart Blueberry Cake 42
- Best Cake Batter Cupcakes 44
- Red Delicious Cupcakes 46
- Double Chocolate Dream 48
- Vanilla Orange Pop-Ups 50
- Carrot Supreme Cupcakes 52
- Hot Chocolate Delight 54
- Bright Rainbow Cupcakes 56
- Sweet Cupcake Poppers 58
- Secret Center Cupcakes 60
- Lemon Drop Cupcakes 62
- Mint Cream Cupcakes 64
- Berry Chocolate Delight 66
- Jelly & Peanut Butter Pops 68
- Hidden Heart Cupcakes 70
- Tasty Pudding Poppers 72
- Cookie Dough Surprise 74

COOKIES & BARS 76
- Classic Chocolate Chip Cookies 78
- Oatmeal Raisin Cookies 80
- Scrumptious Sand Tarts 82
- Choco-Wakka Cookies 84
- Apricot Cookies 86
- Surprise Meringues 88
- Christmas Cochinitos 90
- Bodacious Brownies 92
- Terrific Turtle Bars 94
- Sweet S'mores Bars 96

PIES & TARTS 98
- Basic Pie & Tart Shells 100
- Amazing Apple Pie 104
- Pretty as a Pecan Pie 106
- French Silk Pie 108
- Mighty Mixed Fruit Pie 110
- Rhubarb Berry Pie 112
- Oh My, Chicken Pie 114
- Scrumptious Fruit Tart 116
- Glorious Ginger Pear Tart 118

MUFFINS & QUICK BREADS 120
Sweet Blueberry Muffins 122
Marvelous Morning Muffins............... 124
Tasty Oat & Raisin Surprise 126
Zucchini Cocoa-Nut Nibbles 128
Supreme Gran-Apple Snack............... 130
Sweet Cinnamon Muffins.................... 132
Dreamy Chocolaty Muffins 134
Ideal Poppy Seed Muffins 136
Sweet Strawberries & Cream............. 138
Mini Pancake Muffins........................... 140
Banana Chocolate Delight.................. 142
Perfect Cider Donut Pops.................... 144
Spicy Pumpkin Poppers....................... 146
Fluffy Potato Bake Bites 148
Mac & Cheesy Bites............................... 150
Cheesy Pizza Puff Pieces 152
Hearty Eggs & Bacon Brunch 154
Banana Bread.. 156
Zesty Zucchini Bread 158
Country Pumpkin Bread 160
Sweet Potato Bread 162
Marvelous Monkey Bread 164
Molasses Bread in a Can 166
Fruity Flavorful Bread 168
Cool Cornbread...................................... 170
Savory Herb Pull-Aparts....................... 172

YEASTED BREADS................................. 174
Sticky Cinnamon Rolls.......................... 176
Buttery House Rolls.............................. 178
Classic Sandwich Bread 180
Simple Rosemary Bread....................... 182
Morning Muffin Biscuits 184
Pepperoni Pizza Bread......................... 186

GLOSSARY 188

TO LEARN MORE.................................. 189

INDEX 190

PHOTO CREDITS 191

BAKING BASICS

Baking is like a fun chemistry experiment with delicious results! You certainly wouldn't want to eat a handful of flour. But if you mix flour with other ingredients and expose it to heat, you can transform the ingredients into something delicious. Baking depends on chemistry. You have to mix certain ingredients in a certain order. But baking also allows for creativity. The artistry comes in the flavors you add, the shapes you form, and the decorations you create. When it comes to baking, the possibilities are endless!

Rhubarb Berry Pie

Sweet Cupcake Poppers

Savory Herb Pull-Aparts
Cheesy Pizza Puff Pieces
Simple Rosemary Bread
Terrific Turtle Bars

PREPARATION & SAFETY

Preparation is a key element of successful baking. Here are some things to keep in mind.

ASK PERMISSION

- Get permission to use the kitchen, tools, and ingredients.
- If you'd like to do something by yourself, say so. As long as you can do it safely, do it!
- Ask for help when you need it. Professional chefs have *sous chefs*, which means "assistant chefs" in French. You can have one too!

BE PREPARED

- Read the whole recipe before you plan to bake.
- Make sure you have all the ingredients.
- Will there be enough time? For example, cakes need to cool completely before you frost them.
- Gather all the tools and equipment you will need.
- Prepare the pans as directed and preheat the oven.
- Gather the listed ingredients. Sometimes you need prepared ingredients such as chopped nuts or sifted flour. Do those prep jobs as you gather the ingredients.
- Finally, do the recipe steps in the order they are listed.

SAFETY FIRST!

- Set up a cooling rack ahead of time. Make sure it's easy to get from the oven to the cooling rack.
- Ask an adult for help when boiling something or working with hot syrups.
- Always use oven mitts when handling hot pots and pans. The oven is hot too. Don't bump into the racks or the door.
- Choose a small knife. Cut a small amount of food at a time. Always keep your other hand away from the blade. Work slowly and keep your eyes on the knife.
- Tie back long hair.
- Wash your hands before you begin baking. Rub them with soap for 20 seconds before rinsing. Wash them again if you eat, sneeze, cough, take a bathroom break, or touch the trash container.
- Use clean tools and equipment. If you lick a spoon, wash it before using it again.

GERM ALERT

It's so tempting, but you shouldn't eat batter or dough containing raw eggs. Raw eggs may contain salmonella bacteria, which can cause food poisoning. Eating things that contain raw eggs might make you sick. Ask an adult if it's okay to lick bowls, beaters, and spoons.

ALLERGIES

Millions of people have food allergies or food intolerances. Foods that most often cause allergic reactions include milk, eggs, peanuts, tree nuts, and wheat. Common food intolerances include lactose and gluten. Lactose is the sugar in milk. Gluten is the protein in wheat. Baked goods can be a real hazard for people with food allergies or intolerances. So, be aware of any allergies or intolerances when making and serving baked goods.

springform pan

CONVERSION CHART — INGREDIENTS

STANDARD	METRIC
¼ teaspoon	1.25 mL
½ teaspoon	2.5 mL
1 teaspoon	5 mL
1 tablespoon	15 mL
¼ cup	60 mL
⅓ cup	80 mL
½ cup	125 mL
⅔ cup	160 mL
¾ cup	175 mL
1 cup	240 mL
325°F	160°C
350°F	180°C
375°F	190°C
400°F	200°C

CONVERSION CHART — PAN SIZES

STANDARD	METRIC
8 × 8-inch	20 × 20-cm
8-inch round	20-cm round
9-inch round	23-cm round
9 × 5-inch	23 × 13-cm
9 × 13-inch	23 × 33-cm

8 × 8-inch cake pan

measuring spoons

measuring cups

saucepan

INGREDIENTS

These are common ingredients that bakers use.

BAKING SODA & BAKING POWDER

Baking soda and baking powder are common leavening agents. Leavening agents are ingredients that make baked goods rise. Adding too much leavening makes big air bubbles that pop. This makes baked goods flat.

BUTTER & OIL

Always choose unsalted butter for baking. You add salt in most recipes. Using unsalted butter keeps the recipe from having too much salt. Some recipes will call for oil instead of butter. Oils are made by crushing and pressing seeds and other parts of plants. In recipes that call for oil, use canola oil if you can.

CHOCOLATE

Chocolate comes from the bean of the cacao tree. When cocoa beans are processed, the cocoa particles and the cocoa butter are separated. Then they are recombined in different formulas such as semisweet, bittersweet, and milk chocolate. In general, the higher the cocoa content, the stronger the taste. If it is warm or humid, chocolate may bloom. This means a whitish powder has developed on it. Don't worry. It's still okay to eat and to bake with.

CITRUS ZEST

Sometimes recipes call for citrus zest. The zest is the colored part of the citrus fruit's skin. The oils in the skins are very flavorful, so a little zest goes a long way!

EGGS

Eggs come in many sizes. Use large eggs unless the recipe says otherwise. Bring eggs to room temperature before you add them to the batter. Some recipes call for pasteurized eggs. Pasteurized eggs have been exposed to heat. This destroys bacteria in the eggs. Pasteurized eggs are safe to eat uncooked.

EXTRACTS

There are many flavoring extracts used in baking. Some of these are vanilla, almond, and maple. You will probably use vanilla extract most often. Vanilla extract is made from the beans or seedpods of tropical orchids.

FLOUR

In a recipe, the word "flour" means all-purpose wheat flour. But other grains can be ground into flour too. Some of these grains include rye, buckwheat, and corn.

FRUITS & VEGETABLES

Many recipes feature fruits and vegetables. You can use fresh or frozen produce. If you use frozen produce, be sure to thaw it first. Choose fresh produce that is ripe and not bruised. Always wash fruit and vegetables well. Rinse them under cold water. Pat them dry with a towel. Then they won't slip when you cut them.

MILK & CREAM

You can usually use whatever milk you have, whether it is skim, low fat, or whole milk. Substituting usually won't noticeably affect the quality of what you're making. However, use cream and buttermilk if a recipe says to. You can make buttermilk if you don't have any. Put one tablespoon of white vinegar in a measuring cup. Then and add milk until you have one cup of liquid.

NUTS

Nuts, usually walnuts or pecans, add flavor to baked goods. You can buy them already sliced or chopped.

SALT

You may be surprised to see salt in a dessert recipe. Salt is a flavor enhancer. It enhances the flavors in your baked goods, whether they are sweet or savory.

SUGAR

You use several types of sugar for baking. The most common are granulated sugar, brown sugar, and powdered sugar. Sometimes a recipe may call for other sweeteners such as corn syrup, molasses, or honey. If a recipe just says sugar, it means granulated sugar.

THICKENERS

When you make pies with juicy fresh fruit, you need to use a thickener. Otherwise, all that juice makes a soupy mess! Common thickeners for fruit fillings are tapioca powder or flakes, cornstarch, and flour.

TECHNIQUES

These are the techniques that bakers use.

BEATING EGG WHITES

Beating egg whites makes them fluffy. Egg whites won't get fluffy if there is fat, such as yolk, butter, or chocolate, in them. So, use a clean metal bowl and clean beaters. Make sure there is no yolk in the whites. Beat on high speed until the whites reach the desired firmness.

CHILLING DOUGH

Piecrust is easier to roll out when it is cold. Cold dough also makes a flakier crust. Rolling the dough flattens the pieces of cold butter in the dough. These flat pieces of butter create layers in the crust. The butter makes steam as it melts in the oven. The steam helps puff the layers.

CREAMING

Creaming means beating something until it is smooth and creamy. When baking, you often need to cream butter. Unless the recipe says otherwise, use butter that is near room temperature.

CUTTING IN

Cutting in means working butter into flour until the mixture is crumbly. Use a pastry blender, a fork, or your fingertips.

FLOURING A PAN

Sometimes you will need to flour a pan after you grease it. This stops grease from soaking into baked goods and makes it easier to remove them from the pan. Sprinkle about a tablespoon of flour in the greased pan. Hold the pan with one hand over the sink. Tap its side firmly with the other hand. As you tap, twist and turn the pan to move the flour around. When all the surfaces are lightly coated, dump out the extra flour.

FROSTING CAKES & CUPCAKES

Fill a plastic bag with frosting. Press out the extra air. Seal the bag closed. Pinch one corner of the bag flat. Cut off the corner. You can cut it straight across, or in a V shape or M shape. This is the bag's tip. Hold the bag with the tip pointed down. Squeeze the bag to push out the frosting. Start on the outside edge of the cupcake. Go around the edge. When you reach the beginning of the circle, keep going. Make smaller and smaller circles. This creates a spiral. Stop squeezing when finished.

GREASING A PAN

Butter wrappers are great for greasing pans. If you don't have one, use waxed paper and a bit of butter. Run the paper and butter all around the inside of the pan. There should be a light coating of butter on the bottom and sides.

MEASURING DRY INGREDIENTS

Some ingredients are measured by weight in ounces and pounds (grams and kilograms). The weight is printed on the package label. Many ingredients are measured by the cup, tablespoon, or teaspoon. Measuring tools come in many sizes, but the amount they measure should be printed or etched on the sides of the tools. Dip the measuring spoon or measuring cup into whatever you're measuring. Use a butter knife to scrape off the excess.

MELTING CHOCOLATE

To melt chocolate on the stove, use a double boiler. Put a little water in the bottom part. Put the chocolate in the top part. Turn the burner on low. Simmer the water until the chocolate melts. Stir often. To melt chocolate in a microwave, use medium power. After 30 seconds, stir the chocolate. Then heat it again for another 30 seconds. You may have to do this several times before all the chocolate melts.

MIXING DRY INGREDIENTS

Unless the recipe says otherwise, always stir the dry ingredients together first. Measure them into a bowl and stir them with a fork or a whisk.

REMOVING A BREAD LOAF FROM A PAN

Cool the loaf according to the directions in the recipe. Insert a knife between the loaf and the side of the pan. Run it all the way around the loaf once. Turn the loaf pan upside down on top of the rack. Lightly tap the pan. Then lift it off of the loaf.

REMOVING A CAKE FROM A PAN

Put the cake pan on a cooling rack for about 5 minutes. Insert a knife between the cake and the side of the pan. Run it all the way around the cake. Put the cooling rack upside down on the top of the cake pan. Carefully hold the rack against the cake pan and turn them over together. Lightly tap the cake pan. Then lift it off of the cake. Always let a cake cool completely before frosting it.

ROLLING OUT DOUGH

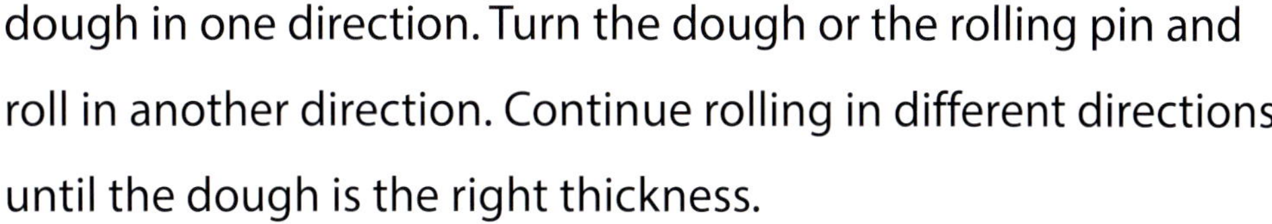

Shape the dough into a disc. Place it on a floured countertop or pastry cloth. Roll the dough in one direction. Turn the dough or the rolling pin and roll in another direction. Continue rolling in different directions until the dough is the right thickness.

SCRAPING A BOWL

When using an electric mixer, turn off the mixer occasionally and scrape the sides. Then scrape the bottom of the bowl with a silicone spatula. That way you'll be sure that all of the ingredients are completely mixed. Recipes don't usually mention this important step. You just have to remember to do it!

SEPARATING AN EGG

Rap the egg firmly on the countertop. Hold the egg over a bowl and pull the shell apart. Gently pass the egg back and forth between the pieces of shell. The white will fall into the bowl. The yolk will remain in the shell.

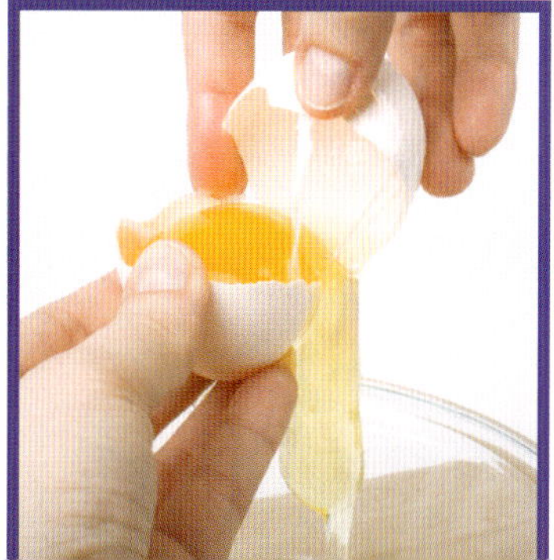

TESTING A BREAD LOAF FOR DONENESS

Remove the pan from the oven. Stick a tester into the center of the loaf and pull it back out. You can use a knife, a wooden skewer, or a toothpick. If no gooey batter sticks to the tester, the bread is done. If the bread isn't done, put it back in the oven. Check it again in a few minutes.

TESTING A CAKE FOR DONENESS

There are three ways to check whether a cake is done. First, remove the cake from the oven. Gently tap the middle of the cake. It will spring back up if it is done. Examine the edges of the cake. They will pull away from the sides of the pan when the cake is done. Stick a tester into the center of the cake and pull it back out. You can use a knife, a wooden skewer, or a toothpick. If no gooey batter sticks to the tester, the cake is done. If the cake isn't done, put it back in the oven. Check it again in a few minutes.

WHIPPING CREAM

Pour the whipping cream into a chilled bowl with deep sides. Beat on high speed until the cream forms peaks. Don't overbeat, or you will make butter!

ZESTING CITRUS FRUIT

Gently scrape the fruit over the small holes of a grater or citrus zester. Remove just the colored part of the skin. Then chop the zest with a small knife. The pieces should be no longer than ¼ inch (0.6 cm).

GLASS OR METAL PANS?

Should you use glass or metal baking pans? Light-colored metal or dark-colored metal? The simple answer is to use whatever is available in your kitchen. But the material and the color do make a difference. Food bakes faster in glass and dark metal pans. If you can, use a light-colored baking sheet for cookies. Cookies will brown more if they are baked on a dark-colored baking sheet.

CAKES & CUPCAKES

Cakes are soft, sweet baked goods made by combining flour, eggs, fat, and sugar. Cakes and cupcakes are versatile desserts. Cakes can have one layer or many. You can top both cakes and cupcakes with icing, whipped cream, powdered sugar, or nothing at all.

Double Chocolate Dream

Mint Cream Cupcakes

Chocolate Flourless Cake

Bright Rainbow Cupcakes
Vanilla Orange
Pop-Ups
Hot Chocolate
Delight

LUSCIOUS LEMON POUND CAKE

makes 8 to 10 servings

INGREDIENTS

- 2 cups flour
- ½ teaspoon salt
- ½ teaspoon baking powder
- 1 cup butter
- 1½ cups sugar
- 3 eggs
- 1 teaspoon lemon extract
- zest of 1 lemon, finely grated
- 1 cup of milk at room temperature
- ice cream & fresh berries (optional)

TOOLS & EQUIPMENT

- 9 × 5-inch loaf pan
- measuring cups
- measuring spoons
- mixing bowls
- whisk
- electric mixer
- zester or grater
- silicone spatula
- wooden skewer
- cooling rack
- knife

1. Grease and flour the loaf pan and set it aside. Preheat the oven to 350 degrees.
2. Whisk together the flour, salt, and baking powder. Set this bowl aside.
3. Put the butter and sugar in another mixing bowl. Beat until light and fluffy.
4. Add the eggs one at a time. Beat for about 1 minute after adding each egg. Then beat in the lemon extract and the lemon zest.
5. Add about one-third of the flour mixture and about one-third of the milk. Beat on low speed just until mixed.
6. Add half of the remaining flour mixture and half of the remaining milk. Beat on low speed just until mixed. Then add the remaining flour mixture and milk. Beat on low just until mixed.
7. Scrape the batter into the prepared loaf pan using the silicone spatula. Bake for about 60 to 75 minutes. Insert a wooden skewer to check for doneness. Crumbs will stick to the skewer when the cake is done.
8. Place the pan on the cooling rack for about 30 minutes. Then remove the cake from the pan and let it cool completely on the rack.
9. To serve, cut the cake into slices about 1 inch (2.5 cm) thick. Serve the cake plain or with ice cream and fresh berries.

HEAVENLY ANGEL FOOD CAKE

makes 10 servings

INGREDIENTS

- 1 angel food cake mix, plus ingredients listed on its box
- 1 pint heavy whipping cream
- 2 tablespoons powdered sugar, sifted
- 1 teaspoon vanilla extract
- 2 cups strawberries, blueberries, or raspberries, rinsed and drained
- chocolate sauce (optional)

TOOLS & EQUIPMENT

- tube pan
- glass bottle (optional)
- knife
- serving platter
- mixing bowl
- electric mixer
- measuring spoons
- sifter
- silicone spatula
- measuring cups

1. Make the cake following the directions on the package.
2. Remove the cake from the oven. Set the pan upside down on its feet or hang it on the neck of a glass bottle. Let the cake cool completely before removing it from the pan. Place the cake on a large, round platter.
3. Wait until you are just about ready to serve the cake. Then whip the cream until it starts thickening. Sprinkle on the powdered sugar and pour in the vanilla. Then continue beating on high speed until the cream is fluffy. Remember not to overbeat the cream!
4. Use a silicone spatula to spread the whipped cream all over the cake.
5. Arrange the berries on top of the cake and around the bottom edge. If you like, drizzle chocolate sauce over the top of the cake.

TRY THIS

Here's how to avoid flattening an angel food cake when you cut it. Use a serrated knife and hold it straight up and down. Using a gentle sawing motion, cut from the center out to the edge of the cake.

TUNNEL OF FUDGE CAKE

makes 12 servings

INGREDIENTS

FOR THE CAKE

2¼ cups flour

¾ cup unsweetened cocoa powder, plus extra for preparing the pan

2 cups chopped walnuts

1¾ cups (3½ sticks) butter

1¾ cups sugar

6 eggs

2 cups powdered sugar

FOR THE GLAZE

¾ cup powdered sugar

¼ cup unsweetened cocoa powder

¼ to ¾ cup milk

TOOLS & EQUIPMENT

Bundt pan	**mixing spoon**
measuring cups	**silicone spatula**
mixing bowls	**cooling rack**
whisk	**serving platter**
electric mixer	**spoon**

1. Grease the pan and "flour" it thoroughly with cocoa powder. The cake will stick to any area that isn't coated. Set the pan aside. Preheat the oven to 350 degrees.

2. Put the flour and the cocoa powder in a mixing bowl. Stir with a whisk to combine them. Stir in the chopped walnuts. Set this bowl aside.

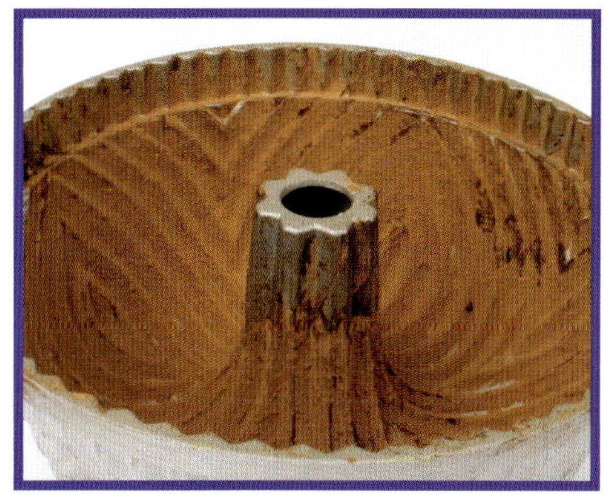

3. Cream the butter. Then beat in the sugar until the mixture is light and fluffy. Add the eggs one at a time. Beat well after you add each one.
4. With the electric mixer on low speed, gradually pour in the powdered sugar. Continue beating until the batter is well blended.
5. Pour the flour and nut mixture into the batter. Stir with a mixing spoon until all of the flour is mixed in.
6. Pour the batter into the prepared pan. Smooth the top of the batter with a silicone spatula.
7. Bake for 45 minutes or until the cake pulls away from the sides of the pan. Set the pan on the cooling rack. Let the cake cool in the pan for 90 minutes.
8. Place a serving platter upside down over the top of the cake pan. Carefully turn the platter and the pan over together. Gently remove the cake pan. Let the cake cool completely for another 2 hours.
9. Make the glaze in a small mixing bowl. Whisk together the powdered sugar, cocoa powder, and half of the milk. If the glaze is too thick to drizzle, add a little more milk.
10. Use a spoon to drizzle the glaze over the cake.

CHOCOLATE FLOURLESS CAKE

makes 8 to 10 servings

INGREDIENTS

- 4 ounces (113 g) bittersweet (not unsweetened) chocolate chips
- ½ cup butter
- ¾ cup sugar
- 3 large eggs
- 1 teaspoon vanilla extract
- ½ cup unsweetened cocoa powder
- powdered sugar
- chocolate sauce (optional)
- raspberries (optional)

TOOLS & EQUIPMENT

- 8-inch round cake pan
- waxed paper
- pencil
- scissors
- double boiler
- measuring cups
- measuring spoons
- mixing spoon
- mixing bowl
- whisk
- sifter
- silicone spatula
- cooling rack
- knife
- serving platter

1. Trace the bottom of the cake pan on waxed paper. Cut out the circle. Grease the cake pan. Place the circle of waxed paper in the bottom of the pan. Grease the waxed paper. Set the pan aside. Preheat the oven to 375 degrees.

2. Set up the double boiler. Melt the chocolate and butter over low heat. Stir occasionally as they melt. Remove the melted chocolate mixture from the heat.

3. In a mixing bowl, whisk together the sugar, eggs, and vanilla. Pour in the chocolate mixture and whisk until blended.
4. Sift the cocoa powder into the mixture and whisk just until combined.

5. Pour the cake batter into the prepared pan. Bake for 25 minutes. Leave the cake in the pan. Place it on a cooling rack for 5 minutes.
6. Run a knife around the edge of the pan. Next, place the serving platter upside down on the cake pan. Carefully turn the platter and cake pan over together. The pan will be on top of the plate. Remove the cake pan and gently peel away the waxed paper.

7. Put some powdered sugar in the sifter. Tap the side gently while moving it around over the cake. If you like, drizzle some chocolate sauce over the top. Try serving it with fresh raspberries!

BERRY SHORTCAKE

makes 6 servings

INGREDIENTS

FOR THE CAKE

2 cups flour
¼ cup sugar
2 teaspoons baking powder
1 teaspoon salt
⅓ cup cold butter, cut into small pieces
¾ cup milk

FOR THE FRUIT

1 pint strawberries, cleaned and cut in half
1 pint blueberries, cleaned and drained
1 tablespoon sugar

FOR THE WHIPPED CREAM

1 cup whipping cream
1 tablespoon sugar

TOOLS & EQUIPMENT

measuring cups
measuring spoons
mixing bowls
whisk
pastry blender
fork
rolling pin
4-inch (10-cm) biscuit cutter or large drinking glass
baking sheet
cooling rack
spatula
serrated knife
cutting board
electric mixer
spoon
dessert plates

1. Preheat the oven to 450 degrees.
2. Whisk together the flour, sugar, baking powder, and salt. Use your fingertips or a pastry blender to cut in the butter. Stop when the mixture looks like coarse crumbs.
3. Use a fork to stir in the milk. Stop stirring when the dough forms a ball.
4. Place the dough on a lightly floured countertop. Knead it for about 1 minute until it is smooth.
5. Roll out the dough to form a rectangle that is ½ inch (1.3 cm) thick. Use the biscuit cutter or a large drinking glass to cut out six circles. Place them on an ungreased baking sheet. Bake for about 10 minutes or until they are lightly browned.
6. Place the shortcakes on a cooling rack. When they are cool, slice each one in half crosswise.
7. Put the strawberry halves and blueberries in a bowl. Add the sugar. Stir to coat the fruit with the sugar. Set this bowl aside.
8. Make the whipped cream right before you are ready to serve the shortcakes. Place the whipping cream and the sugar in a mixing bowl. Beat the cream until it forms stiff peaks. Do not overbeat.
9. Place the bottom half of a shortcake on a dessert plate. Place a spoonful of whipped cream on the shortcake. Top the whipped cream with a spoonful of fruit. Place the top half of the shortcake over the fruit. Top with a small dollop of whipped cream.

HONEY NUT CAKE

makes about 16 servings

INGREDIENTS

FOR THE CAKE

½ cup matzoh meal
½ teaspoon cinnamon
¼ teaspoon salt
¾ cup sugar
¼ cup packed brown sugar
¼ cup vegetable oil
3 eggs
3 tablespoons orange juice
½ cup finely chopped almonds
1 cup finely chopped walnuts

FOR THE SYRUP

⅔ cup sugar
¼ cup honey
⅓ cup orange juice
1 tablespoon lemon juice
¼ cup water
¼ teaspoon cinnamon

TOOLS & EQUIPMENT

8 × 8-inch cake pan
measuring cups
measuring spoons
mixing bowls
whisk
mixing spoon
cooling rack
small saucepan
fork

1. Preheat the oven to 350 degrees. Grease the cake pan and set it aside.
2. Whisk together the matzoh meal, cinnamon, and salt. Set this bowl aside.
3. Whisk together the sugar, brown sugar, vegetable oil, eggs, and orange juice.
4. Stir the matzoh mixture into the egg mixture. Then stir in the almonds and walnuts.
5. Pour the batter into the prepared pan. Bake for 35 to 40 minutes. The top will be light brown and firm. Place the pan on a cooling rack and let the cake cool completely.
6. While the cake cools, make the syrup. Place the sugar, honey, orange juice, lemon juice, water, and cinnamon in a small saucepan. Simmer the mixture, stirring it occasionally. Let it simmer until it is syrupy and all the sugar has dissolved. This takes about 10 minutes. Take the pan off the heat and let the syrup cool.
7. Use a fork to poke holes all over the top of the cake. Slowly pour the cooled syrup over the top of the cake. The syrup should soak into the cake, not run off. If it runs off, pour more slowly or poke more holes in the cake.
8. Refrigerate the cake for at least 4 hours before cutting it. This cake is very sweet, so cut small pieces!

FESTIVE APPLE KUCHEN

makes 10 servings

INGREDIENTS

FOR THE CRUST

- 1 cup flour
- ¼ teaspoon salt
- ¼ teaspoon cinnamon
- ⅓ cup butter, cut into small pieces
- ¼ cup sour cream

FOR THE TOPPING

- 3 cups of peeled, cored, and sliced apples
- ½ cup sour cream
- 3 egg yolks
- 1 cup sugar
- ¼ cup flour
- 1 teaspoon vanilla

TOOLS & EQUIPMENT

- 9-inch springform pan
- measuring cups
- measuring spoons
- mixing bowls
- whisk
- pastry blender
- mixing spoon
- cooling rack
- knife

1. Preheat the oven to 350 degrees. Grease the pan and set it aside.

2. Put the flour, salt, and cinnamon in a bowl and whisk them together. Add the butter. Cut it into the flour with your fingertips or a pastry blender. When the mixture looks like small crumbs, stir in ¼ cup of sour cream.

3. Press the mixture evenly over the bottom of the pan. Bake the crust about 20 to 25 minutes, or until it is lightly browned. Put the pan on a cooling rack and let it cool slightly.

4. For the topping, arrange the apple slices on the crust.

5. Whisk together the sour cream, egg yolks, sugar, flour, and vanilla. Pour this mixture over the apples.

6. Bake the kuchen for about 45 minutes. Test the kuchen for doneness. When a knife tip inserted into the center comes out clean, it is done.

7. Put the pan on a cooling rack until it is cool enough to handle. Release the clasp on the side of the pan and lift it off. You can leave the kuchen on the bottom of the pan.

VELVETY CHOCOLATE CAKE

makes 12 servings

INGREDIENTS

FOR THE CAKE

2 cups flour
2 cups sugar
½ teaspoon cinnamon
¼ teaspoon salt
1 cup butter
½ cup cocoa powder
1 cup hot water
½ cup buttermilk
2 eggs
1 teaspoon baking soda
1¼ teaspoon vanilla extract

FOR THE FROSTING

½ cup butter, melted
6 tablespoons buttermilk
4 cups powdered sugar
1½ teaspoon vanilla extract

TOOLS & EQUIPMENT

measuring cups
measuring spoons
mixing bowls
mixing spoons
saucepan
whisk
8 × 8-inch baking dish
silicone spatula

1. Preheat the oven to 350 degrees. Put the flour, sugar, cinnamon, and salt in a large mixing bowl. Stir well. Set this bowl aside.
2. Melt the butter in a saucepan. Stir in the cocoa powder and hot water. Heat the mixture for 30 seconds. Pour the butter mixture over the flour mixture. Stir well.
3. Add the buttermilk, eggs, baking soda, and vanilla extract. Whisk together.
4. Pour the batter into the baking dish. Spread it evenly with a silicone spatula. Bake 20 minutes. Let the cake cool.
5. In a small mixing bowl, whisk together the frosting ingredients. Pour the frosting over the cake. Spread it evenly with a silicone spatula.

TART BLUEBERRY CAKE

makes 9 servings

INGREDIENTS

- non-stick cooking spray
- ½ cup butter
- 1 cup sugar
- ¼ teaspoon salt
- 2 teaspoons vanilla extract
- 2 eggs
- 1 teaspoon baking powder
- 1½ cup plus 1 tablespoon flour
- 1½ cup blueberries
- 2 tablespoons brown sugar

TOOLS & EQUIPMENT

- 8 × 8-inch baking dish
- measuring cups
- measuring spoons
- mixing bowls
- electric mixer
- mixing spoon
- whisk

1. Preheat the oven to 350 degrees. Grease the baking dish with non-stick cooking spray and set it aside.
2. Cream the butter and ½ cup sugar in a large mixing bowl. Add the salt and vanilla extract. Stir.
3. Separate the eggs. Put the whites in a small bowl. Set them aside. Add the yolks to the butter mixture. Whisk until creamy.
4. Stir the baking powder and 1½ cups flour into the butter mixture.
5. Put the berries and 1 tablespoon flour in a small mixing bowl. Stir to coat the berries with flour. Add the berries to the batter. Stir to mix in the berries.
6. Whisk the egg whites until they are thick. Whisk in the remaining sugar one tablespoon at a time. Add the egg mixture to the batter. Stir well.
7. Pour the batter into the baking dish. Sprinkle the brown sugar over the top. Bake 50 minutes.

BEST CAKE BATTER CUPCAKES

makes 24 cupcakes

INGREDIENTS

FOR THE CUPCAKES

1 18-ounce (510-g) yellow sprinkle cake mix
¼ cup vegetable oil
1 cup buttermilk
4 eggs
1 teaspoon vanilla extract
¼ cup multicolored sprinkles

FOR THE FROSTING

½ cup unsalted butter, softened
2 cups powdered sugar
½ cup yellow sprinkle cake mix
1 teaspoon vanilla extract
1 tablespoon whole milk

1. Preheat the oven to 350 degrees. Put paper liners in the muffin tins.
2. In a large mixing bowl, whisk together the cake mix, oil, buttermilk, eggs, and vanilla extract. Add the sprinkles. Stir lightly.
3. Divide the batter evenly between the paper liners. Bake and cool as directed on the cake mix box.
4. Make the frosting. Put the butter and sugar in a medium bowl. Beat with an electric mixer until creamy. Mix in the cake mix, vanilla extract, and milk.
5. Remove the cupcakes from the muffin tins. Frost the cupcakes. Sprinkle multicolored sprinkles on top.

TOOLS & EQUIPMENT

paper liners
2 muffin tins
mixing bowls
whisk
measuring cups
measuring spoons
scoop
electric mixer
silicone spatula
plastic bag

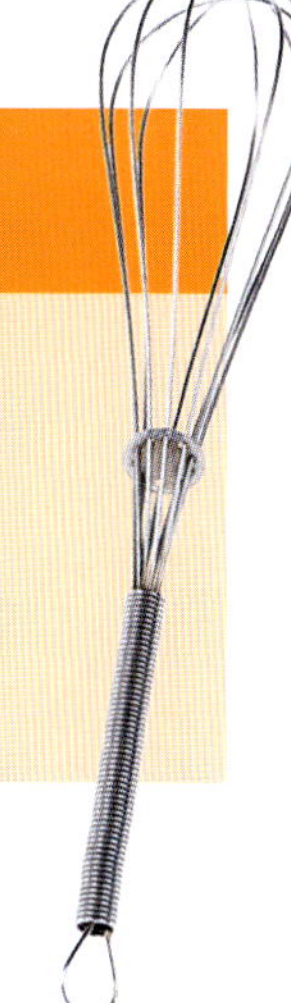

RED DELICIOUS CUPCAKES

makes 24 cupcakes

INGREDIENTS

FOR THE CUPCAKES

1 18.5-ounce (524-g) German chocolate cake mix

½ cup unsalted butter, softened

1 cup buttermilk

½ cup water

½ cup vegetable oil

2 eggs

1 tablespoon unsweetened cocoa powder

10 drops red food coloring

FOR THE FROSTING

½ cup unsalted butter, softened

1 8-ounce (227-g) package cream cheese

2 cups powdered sugar

1 teaspoon vanilla extract

TOOLS & EQUIPMENT

paper liners
2 muffin tins
measuring cups
measuring spoons
mixing bowls
electric mixer
scoop
silicone spatula
plastic bag

1. Preheat the oven to 350 degrees. Put paper liners in the muffin tins.
2. Put all of the cupcake ingredients in a large mixing bowl. Beat with an electric mixer.
3. Divide the batter evenly between the paper liners. Bake and cool as directed on the cake mix box.
4. Make the frosting. Put the butter and cream cheese in a medium bowl. Beat with an electric mixer until creamy. Mix in the powdered sugar and vanilla extract.
5. Remove the cupcakes from the muffin tins. Frost the cupcakes.

DOUBLE CHOCOLATE DREAM

makes 24 cupcakes

INGREDIENTS

FOR THE CUPCAKES

1 18-ounce (510-g) chocolate cake mix

1 cup mayonnaise

1 cup water

3 eggs

FOR THE FROSTING

2 cups unsalted butter, softened

5 cups powdered sugar

2 teaspoons vanilla extract

½ cup semisweet chocolate chips, melted

chocolate sprinkles

1. Preheat the oven to 350 degrees. Put paper liners in the muffin tins.
2. Put all of the cupcake ingredients in a large mixing bowl. Beat with an electric mixer.
3. Divide the batter evenly between the paper liners. Bake and cool as directed on the cake mix box.
4. Make the frosting. Put the butter, sugar, vanilla extract, and melted chocolate in a medium bowl. Beat with an electric mixer until creamy.
5. Remove the cupcakes from the muffin tins. Use a knife to frost the cupcakes. Roll the tops of the cupcakes in the sprinkles.

TOOLS & EQUIPMENT

paper liners
2 muffin tins
measuring cups
measuring spoons
mixing bowls
silicone spatula
electric mixer
scoop
knife
small bowl

VANILLA ORANGE POP-UPS

makes 62 cupcakes

INGREDIENTS

FOR THE CUPCAKES

1 18-ounce (510-g) white cake mix
1 package vanilla pudding mix
1 package orange gelatin
1¼ cups orange juice
⅓ cup vegetable oil
4 eggs
1 teaspoon vanilla extract

FOR THE FROSTING

1 cup unsalted butter, softened
6 cups powdered sugar
¼ cup orange juice
1 teaspoon vanilla extract
¼ teaspoon orange extract
2 to 3 drops of orange food coloring

1. Preheat the oven to 350 degrees. Put paper liners in the muffin tins.
2. In a large mixing bowl, whisk together all of the cupcake ingredients.
3. Divide the batter evenly between the paper liners. Bake and cool as directed on the cake mix box.
4. Make the frosting. Put the butter and sugar in a medium bowl. Beat with an electric mixer until creamy. Mix in the juice, vanilla extract, orange extract, and food coloring.
5. Remove the cupcakes from the muffin tins. Frost the cupcakes.

TOOLS & EQUIPMENT

paper liners
mini muffin tins
measuring cups
measuring spoons
mixing bowls
whisk
scoop
electric mixer
silicone spatula
plastic bag

CARROT SUPREME CUPCAKES

makes 24 cupcakes

INGREDIENTS

FOR THE CUPCAKES

1 18-ounce (510-g) carrot cake mix

1 cup buttermilk

½ cup vegetable oil

4 eggs

½ teaspoon nutmeg

½ teaspoon cinnamon

FOR THE FROSTING

½ cup unsalted butter, softened

1 8-ounce (227-g) package cream cheese

2 cups powdered sugar

1 teaspoon vanilla extract

1. Preheat the oven to 350 degrees. Put paper liners in the muffin tins.
2. Put all of the cupcake ingredients in a large mixing bowl. Stir with a whisk.
3. Fill the paper liners two-thirds full of batter. Bake and cool as directed on the cake mix box.
4. Make the frosting. Put the butter and cream cheese in a medium bowl. Beat with an electric mixer until creamy. Mix in the powdered sugar and vanilla extract.
5. Remove the cupcakes from the muffin tins. Frost the cupcakes.

TOOLS & EQUIPMENT

paper liners
2 muffin tins
measuring cups
measuring spoons
mixing bowls
whisk
scoop
electric mixer
silicone spatula
plastic bag

HOT CHOCOLATE DELIGHT

makes 4 servings

INGREDIENTS

- 8 ounces (227 g) unsalted butter, softened
- 1 ounce (28 g) unsweetened chocolate chips
- 6 ounces (170 g) milk chocolate chips
- ¾ cup all-purpose flour
- ¾ cup sugar
- ½ teaspoon vanilla extract
- 1 teaspoon unsweetened cocoa powder
- 1 teaspoon salt
- 4 eggs
- whipped cream
- mini marshmallows

1. Put the butter, unsweetened chocolate chips, and milk chocolate chips in a microwave-safe bowl. Microwave on high 1 minute. Stir and set the bowl aside.
2. In a medium mixing bowl, whisk together the flour, sugar, vanilla extract, cocoa powder, salt, and eggs.
3. Add the chocolate mixture to the flour mixture. Whisk together.
4. Use a ladle to divide batter evenly between the mugs. Microwave them one at a time on high for 2 minutes. Let them cool 1 minute.
5. Top each mug with whipped cream and mini marshmallows.

TOOLS & EQUIPMENT

- microwave-safe bowl
- mixing spoon
- medium bowl
- measuring cups
- measuring spoons
- whisk
- ladle
- 4 large microwave-safe mugs

BRIGHT RAINBOW CUPCAKES

makes 24 cupcakes

INGREDIENTS

- 1 18.5-ounce (524-g) white cake mix
- 2 eggs
- 1 cup sour cream
- ½ cup whole milk
- ⅓ cup vegetable oil
- food coloring (red, yellow, green & blue)
- whipped cream

1. Preheat the oven to 350 degrees. Put paper liners in the muffin tins.
2. In a large mixing bowl, whisk together the cake mix, eggs, sour cream, milk, and oil.
3. Divide the batter evenly between the five cereal bowls.
4. Add 17 drops of red food coloring to one bowl. Add 13 drops of yellow and 4 drops of red to the second bowl. Add 12 drops of yellow to the third bowl. Add 12 drops of green to the fourth bowl. Add 12 drops of blue to the fifth bowl. Stir each bowl with a different spoon.
5. Put 2 teaspoons of blue batter in each paper liner. Gently spread the batter evenly. Repeat with the other colors, going in reverse rainbow order.
6. Bake and cool the cupcakes as directed on the cake mix box. Top the cupcakes with whipped cream.

TOOLS & EQUIPMENT

paper liners
2 muffin tins
large mixing bowl
measuring cups
measuring spoons
whisk
5 cereal bowls
5 spoons

SWEET CUPCAKE POPPERS

makes 24 cupcakes

INGREDIENTS

- non-stick cooking spray
- ¾ cup unsweetened cocoa powder
- ¾ cup all-purpose flour
- ½ teaspoon baking soda
- ¼ teaspoon salt
- ¾ cup unsalted butter, softened
- 1 cup sugar
- 3 eggs
- 1 teaspoon vanilla extract
- ½ cup sour cream
- 2 cups white chocolate chips
- ½ cup multicolored sprinkles

1. Preheat the oven to 350 degrees. Grease the muffin tin with non-stick cooking spray.
2. In a large mixing bowl, whisk together the cocoa powder, flour, baking soda, and salt. Put the butter, sugar, eggs, vanilla extract, and sour cream in a medium bowl. Stir. Add the butter mixture to the cocoa powder mixture. Stir well.
3. Fill the muffin cups three-fourths full of batter. Bake 10 to 12 minutes. Let the cupcakes cool.

4. Put the white chocolate chips in a microwave-safe bowl. Microwave for 1 minute. Stir. Repeat until the chocolate is melted. Put the sprinkles in a small bowl. Dip the top of each cupcake in the melted chocolate and then in the sprinkles. Chill the cupcakes in the refrigerator 5 minutes.
5. Dip the end of a lollipop stick in the melted chocolate. Push it into the bottom of a cupcake. Repeat until there is a stick in each cupcake. Chill the cupcakes in the refrigerator 5 minutes.

TOOLS & EQUIPMENT

mini muffin tin
mixing bowls
measuring cups
measuring spoons
whisk
mixing spoon
scoop
microwave-safe bowl
small bowl
plastic lollipop stick

SECRET CENTER CUPCAKES

makes 12 cupcakes

INGREDIENTS

FOR THE CUPCAKES

1½ cups flour
½ teaspoon salt
1 teaspoon baking soda
¼ cup unsweetened cocoa powder
⅓ cup vegetable oil
1 cup water
1 cup sugar
1 tablespoon white vinegar
1 teaspoon vanilla extract

FOR THE FILLING

8 ounces (227 g) cream cheese at room temperature
1 egg
½ teaspoon salt
⅓ cup sugar
1 cup chocolate chips

FOR THE TOPPING

2 teaspoons cinnamon
2 teaspoons sugar
¼ cup sliced almonds

TOOLS & EQUIPMENT

muffin tin
paper liners
mixing bowls
measuring cups
measuring spoons
whisk
mixing spoon
electric mixer
silicone spatula
scoop
cooling rack

1. Preheat the oven to 350 degrees. Put paper liners in the muffin tin.
2. In a mixing bowl, whisk together the flour, salt, baking soda, and cocoa powder. Set this bowl aside.
3. In another mixing bowl, whisk together the vegetable oil, water, sugar, vinegar, and vanilla extract. Stir in the flour mixture. Mix with a mixing spoon until the batter is smooth. Set this bowl aside.
4. For the filling, put the cream cheese, egg, salt, and sugar in a small mixing bowl. Beat just until smooth. Stir in the chocolate chips.
5. Fill each paper liner half full with chocolate batter. Then drop a small spoonful of cream cheese filling on top of the batter. The batter will rise around the filling when you bake the cupcakes.
6. For the topping, stir together the cinnamon and sugar. Place a few almond slices on top of each cupcake. Then sprinkle a little of the cinnamon-sugar over the almonds.
7. Bake for about 35 minutes. Cool the cupcakes on a rack for about 10 minutes. Then remove them from the pan. Leave the cupcakes on the rack until they are completely cool.

LEMON DROP CUPCAKES

makes 12 cupcakes

INGREDIENTS

FOR THE CUPCAKES

- 1⅓ cups all-purpose flour
- ¾ tablespoon baking powder
- ¼ teaspoon salt
- ¾ tablespoon lemon zest
- 6 tablespoons unsalted butter, softened
- 1 cup sugar
- 1 egg
- ½ teaspoon vanilla extract
- ½ cup buttermilk
- 1 cup lemon curd

FOR THE FROSTING

- ½ cup unsalted butter, softened
- 1 8-ounce (227-g) package cream cheese
- 2 cups powdered sugar
- 1 teaspoon vanilla extract

1. Preheat the oven to 350 degrees. Put paper liners in the muffin tin. In a large bowl, whisk together the flour, baking powder, and salt. Set this bowl aside.
2. In a medium bowl, whisk the lemon zest, butter, and sugar until fluffy. Mix in the egg, vanilla extract, and buttermilk. Add the butter mixture to the flour mixture. Mix well.
3. Fill the paper liners two-thirds full of batter. Bake 16 minutes. Let the cupcakes cool.
4. Remove the cupcakes from the muffin tins. Use a teaspoon to make a hole in the top of each cupcake. Fill the holes with lemon curd.
5. Make the frosting. Put the butter and cream cheese in a medium bowl. Beat with an electric mixer until creamy. Mix in the powdered sugar and vanilla extract. Frost the cupcakes.

TOOLS & EQUIPMENT

paper liners
muffin tin
mixing bowls
whisk
measuring cups
measuring spoons
zester or grater
silicone spatula
scoop
electric mixer
plastic bag

MINT CREAM CUPCAKES

makes 24 cupcakes

INGREDIENTS

- 1 18.25-ounce (517-g) chocolate cake mix
- 1 box chocolate pudding mix
- 1 cup sour cream
- ½ cup vegetable oil
- 4 eggs
- ½ cup water
- ½ gallon (1.9 L) mint chocolate chip ice cream
- 1 cup heavy whipping cream
- ¾ cup mini semisweet chocolate chips

1. Preheat the oven to 350 degrees. Put foil liners in the muffin tins.
2. In a large mixing bowl, whisk together the cake mix, pudding mix, sour cream, oil, eggs, and water.
3. Put 1 tablespoon of batter in each foil liner. Bake 8 minutes. Let the cupcakes cool 10 minutes. Then put them in the freezer for 30 minutes.
4. Scoop ice cream into the foil liners. Fill each liner to the top. Put the cupcakes back in the freezer for 1 hour.
5. Put the heavy whipping cream in a small saucepan. Heat and stir it until it boils. Remove the pan from the heat. Stir in the chocolate chips. Let the mixture cool.
6. Put a tablespoon of chocolate mixture on each cupcake. Freeze the cupcakes for 20 minutes.

TOOLS & EQUIPMENT

foil liners
2 muffin tins
mixing bowl
whisk
measuring cups
measuring spoons
scoop
small saucepan

BERRY CHOCOLATE DELIGHT

makes 24 cupcakes

INGREDIENTS

FOR THE CUPCAKES

1 18.25-ounce (517-g) vanilla cake mix

1¼ cups buttermilk

⅓ cup vegetable oil

4 eggs

1 teaspoon vanilla extract

24 strawberries

mint leaves

FOR THE FROSTING

1 box chocolate pudding mix

2 cups heavy whipping cream

1. Preheat the oven to 350 degrees. Put paper liners in the muffin tins.
2. In a large mixing bowl, whisk together the cake mix, buttermilk, oil, eggs, and vanilla extract.
3. Fill the paper liners three-fourths full of batter. Bake 18 to 20 minutes. Let the cupcakes cool 15 minutes.
4. Make the frosting. Put the frosting ingredients in a medium bowl. Beat with an electric mixer for 5 minutes.
5. Use a teaspoon to make a hole in the top of each cupcake. Cut the stems off of the strawberries. Put a strawberry in the hole in each cupcake.
6. Frost the cupcakes. Stick mint leaves on top of each cupcake.

TOOLS & EQUIPMENT

paper liners
2 muffin tins
mixing bowls
whisk
measuring cups
measuring spoons
scoop
electric mixer
knife
cutting board
silicone spatula
plastic bag

JELLY & PEANUT BUTTER POPS

makes 24 cupcakes

INGREDIENTS

FOR THE CUPCAKES

- 1⅓ cups all-purpose flour
- ¼ teaspoon baking soda
- ¾ teaspoon baking powder
- ¼ teaspoon salt
- ¾ cup unsalted butter, softened
- 1⅓ cups sugar
- ⅓ cup creamy peanut butter
- 3 eggs
- 1 teaspoon vanilla extract
- ½ cup sour cream
- ½ cup of chopped salted roasted peanuts
- ½ cup strawberry jelly

FOR THE FROSTING

- ½ cup unsalted butter, softened
- 1 cup creamy peanut butter
- 3 tablespoons whole milk
- 2 cups powdered sugar

1. Preheat the oven to 375 degrees. Put paper liners in the muffin tins. In a large mixing bowl, whisk together the flour, baking soda, baking powder, and salt. Set this bowl aside.
2. Put the butter and sugar in a medium bowl. Mix with an electric mixer. Mix in the peanut butter, eggs, and vanilla extract. Add the peanut butter mixture to the flour mixture. Mix for 5 minutes. Mix in the sour cream and peanuts.

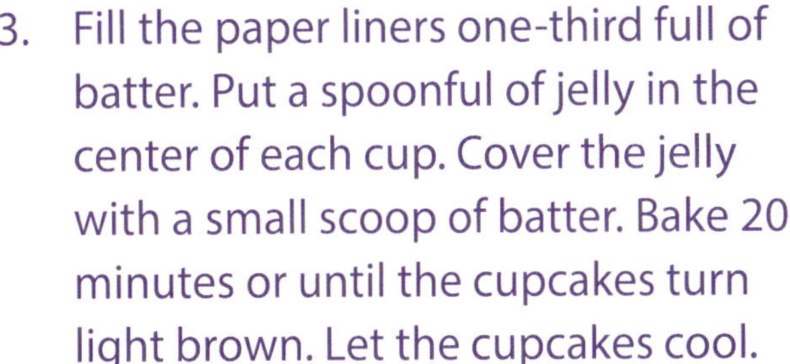

3. Fill the paper liners one-third full of batter. Put a spoonful of jelly in the center of each cup. Cover the jelly with a small scoop of batter. Bake 20 minutes or until the cupcakes turn light brown. Let the cupcakes cool.

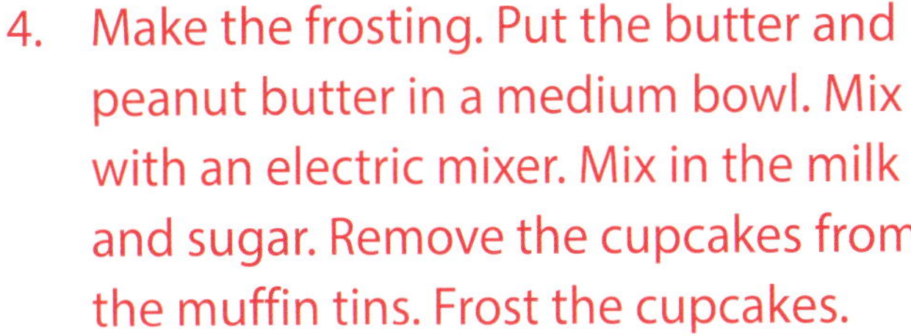

4. Make the frosting. Put the butter and peanut butter in a medium bowl. Mix with an electric mixer. Mix in the milk and sugar. Remove the cupcakes from the muffin tins. Frost the cupcakes.

TOOLS & EQUIPMENT

paper liners
2 muffin tins
mixing bowls
whisk
measuring cups
measuring spoons
electric mixer
scoop
mixing spoon
silicone spatula
plastic bag

HIDDEN HEART CUPCAKES

makes 12 cupcakes

INGREDIENTS

FOR THE CUPCAKES

- non-stick cooking spray
- 1 18.25-ounce (517-g) vanilla cake mix
- 1 cup buttermilk
- ½ cup vegetable oil
- 4 eggs
- red food coloring

FOR THE FROSTING

- ½ cup unsalted butter, softened
- 4 cups powdered sugar
- 1 teaspoon vanilla extract
- 5 tablespoons whole milk

1. Preheat the oven to 350 degrees. Grease the baking pan and muffin tin with non-stick cooking spray.
2. In a large mixing bowl, whisk together the cake mix, buttermilk, oil, and eggs.
3. Put one-third of the batter in a medium bowl. Mix in red food coloring. Add a few drops at a time until it's the color you want. Put the red batter in the baking pan. Bake 8 to 10 minutes. Let the cake cool. Use the cookie cutter to cut 12 heart shapes out of the cake.
4. Put 2 tablespoons of the remaining batter in each muffin cup. Put one cake heart point down in each cup. Press them into the batter. Cover each heart with 1 tablespoon of batter. Bake 15 to 18 minutes. Let the cupcakes cool.
5. Put the frosting ingredients in a medium bowl. Beat with an electric mixer until creamy. Remove the cupcakes from the muffin tins. Use a silicone spatula to frost the cupcakes.

TOOLS & EQUIPMENT

8 × 8-inch baking pan
muffin tin
mixing bowls
measuring cups
measuring spoons
whisk
heart-shaped cookie cutter
electric mixer
silicone spatula

TASTY PUDDING POPPERS

makes 24 cupcakes

INGREDIENTS

FOR THE CUPCAKES

- non-stick cooking spray
- 1 18.25-ounce (517-g) yellow cake mix
- 1 box vanilla pudding mix
- 1 cup sour cream
- ½ cup vegetable oil
- 4 eggs
- ½ cup water

FOR THE FILLING

- 1 box vanilla pudding mix
- 2 cups heavy whipping cream

1. Preheat the oven to 350 degrees. Grease the muffin tins with non-stick cooking spray.
2. In a large mixing bowl, whisk together the cake mix, pudding mix, sour cream, oil, eggs, and water.
3. Fill the muffin cups two-thirds full of batter. Bake 20 minutes. Let the cupcakes cool. Then put them in the freezer for 30 minutes.
4. In a medium bowl, whisk the filling ingredients for 5 minutes.
5. Cut the cupcakes in half horizontally.
6. Put a tablespoon of filling between the halves of each cupcake. Use the rest of the filling to frost the cupcakes.

TOOLS & EQUIPMENT

2 muffin tins
mixing bowls
measuring cups
measuring spoons
whisk
scoop
knife
cutting board
silicone spatula
plastic bag

COOKIE DOUGH SURPRISE

makes 24 cupcakes

INGREDIENTS

FOR THE FILLING

- 4 tablespoons unsalted butter, softened
- 6 tablespoons brown sugar
- 1 cup all-purpose flour
- 1 7-ounce (198-g) can sweetened condensed milk
- ¼ teaspoon vanilla extract
- ¼ cup mini semisweet chocolate chips

FOR THE CUPCAKES

- 1 18.25-ounce (517-g) chocolate cake mix
- 1 cup buttermilk
- ½ cup vegetable oil
- 3 eggs
- 1 teaspoon vanilla extract

FOR THE FROSTING

- ½ cup unsalted butter, softened
- 4 cups powdered sugar
- 5 tablespoons milk
- 2 teaspoons vanilla extract
- ¼ cup mini semisweet chocolate chips

TOOLS & EQUIPMENT

- measuring cups
- measuring spoons
- mixing bowls
- mixing spoon
- parchment paper
- baking sheet
- paper liners
- 2 muffin tins
- whisk
- scoop
- silicone spatula

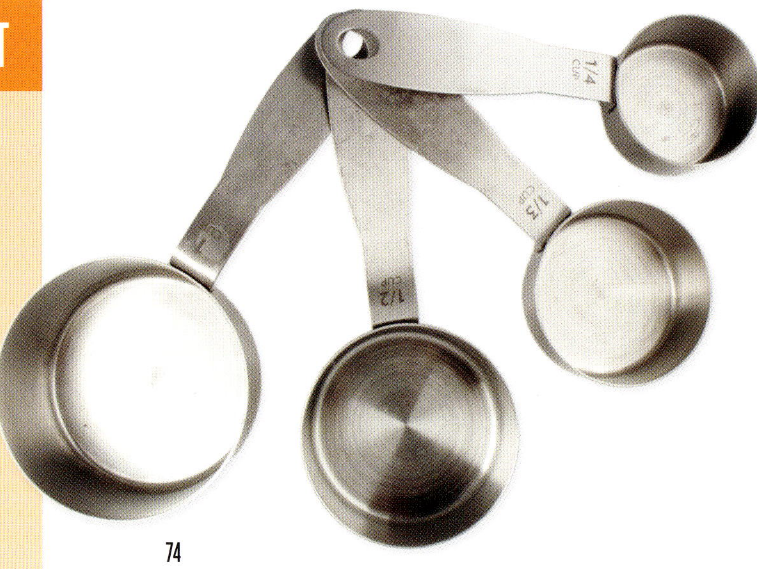

1. Mix all of the filling ingredients together in a medium mixing bowl. Form the dough into 1-inch (2.5-cm) balls and place them on a parchment-lined baking sheet. Put them in the freezer for 2 hours.
2. Preheat the oven to 350 degrees. Put paper liners in the muffin tins.
3. In a large bowl, whisk together the cake mix, buttermilk, oil, eggs and vanilla extract. Fill the paper liners two-thirds full of batter. Place a cookie dough ball in the center of each liner. Bake 17 minutes. Let the cupcakes cool.
4. Make the frosting. In a medium bowl, whisk the butter and sugar until creamy. Mix in the milk and vanilla extract. Remove the cupcakes from the muffin tins. Use a silicone spatula to frost the cupcakes. Top with chocolate chips.

COOKIES & BARS

Cookies are small, flat baked treats that can be crispy or chewy. Bars are desserts baked in pans and cut into squares or rectangles. They are typically softer than cookies but not as soft as cakes.

Oatmeal Raisin Cookies

Surprise Meringues

Scrumptious Sand Tarts
Christmas Cochinitos
Terrific
Turtle Bars

CLASSIC CHOCOLATE CHIP COOKIES

makes about 3 dozen cookies

INGREDIENTS

- 1½ cups flour
- ½ teaspoon baking soda
- ½ teaspoon salt
- ⅔ cup butter, softened
- ½ cup sugar
- ½ cup packed brown sugar
- 1 egg
- 1 teaspoon vanilla extract
- 1 cup semisweet chocolate chips
- ½ cup chopped walnuts (optional)

TOOLS & EQUIPMENT

- mixing bowls
- measuring cups
- measuring spoons
- whisk
- electric mixer
- silicone spatula
- mixing spoon
- dinner spoons
- cookie sheets
- cooling rack
- spatula

1. Preheat the oven to 375 degrees.
2. Whisk together the flour, baking soda, and salt. Set this bowl aside.
3. In another mixing bowl, cream the butter and the sugars. The mixture should be light and fluffy.
4. Beat in the egg and the vanilla extract.

5. Gradually stir the flour mixture into the butter mixture. Then stir in the chocolate chips and the walnuts.
6. Use two dinner spoons to drop dough onto an ungreased cookie sheet. Use one spoon to push the dough off the other. Space the cookies about 2 inches (5 cm) apart.

7. Bake for 8 to 10 minutes. Let the cookies cool on the pan for about 1 minute. Then transfer them to the cooling rack with a spatula.

TRY THIS

- Replace semisweet chocolate chips with peanut butter chips or candy-coated chocolates.
- Use white chocolate chips instead of semisweet chocolate chips. Use macadamia nuts instead of walnuts.
- Ask an adult helper to chop up Mexican chocolate. Use that instead of chocolate chips. Add 2 teaspoons cinnamon, ⅛ teaspoon ground black pepper, and ¼ teaspoon cayenne pepper when you add the vanilla.

OATMEAL RAISIN COOKIES

makes about 5 dozen cookies

INGREDIENTS

2 cups flour
1 teaspoon baking powder
1 teaspoon baking soda
½ teaspoon salt
1 teaspoon cinnamon
¼ teaspoon nutmeg
1⅓ cups butter
2 cups packed brown sugar
⅔ cup sugar, plus 2 tablespoons for topping
2 eggs
1 tablespoon vanilla extract
4 cups quick-cooking oats
1 cup raisins

TOOLS & EQUIPMENT

cookie sheets
mixing bowls
measuring cups
measuring spoons
whisk
electric mixer
mixing spoon
saucer
drinking glass
cooling rack
spatula

1. Preheat the oven to 350 degrees. Grease the cookie sheets and set them aside.
2. Whisk together the flour, baking powder, baking soda, salt, cinnamon, and nutmeg. Set this bowl aside.
3. Cream the butter on medium speed. Add the sugars. Beat until the mixture is fluffy and light.
4. Beat in the eggs and the vanilla extract.
5. Stir in flour mixture.
6. Stir in the oats and the raisins.
7. Roll the dough into 1½-inch (3.8-cm) balls. Place them on the cookie sheets about 3 inches (7.6 cm) apart.
8. Pour 2 tablespoons of sugar into a saucer. Grease the bottom of the drinking glass. Dip the bottom of the glass in the sugar. Flatten a ball of dough with the bottom of the glass. Repeat until all the balls of dough are flattened.
9. Bake for 8 to 10 minutes. Let the cookies cool on the pan for about 2 minutes. Then transfer them to the cooling rack with a spatula.

SCRUMPTIOUS SAND TARTS

makes about 4 dozen cookies

INGREDIENTS

- 1 cup butter
- ½ cup powdered sugar, plus some extra
- 1 teaspoon vanilla extract
- 2 cups flour
- 1 cup chopped pecans

1. Preheat the oven to 325 degrees.
2. Cream the butter. Then beat in the ½ cup of powdered sugar and the vanilla.
3. Stir in the flour and the nuts.
4. Roll the dough into 1-inch (2.5-cm) balls. Place them about 1 inch (2.5 cm) apart on an ungreased cookie sheet. Gently flatten them into disks.
5. Bake for 22 to 25 minutes. Let the cookies cool on the pan for about 2 minutes. Then transfer them to the cooling rack with a spatula. While the cookies are still warm, sift a light coating of powdered sugar over them.

TOOLS & EQUIPMENT

mixing bowl
electric mixer
measuring cups
measuring spoons
mixing spoon
silicone spatula
cookie sheets
spatula
cooling rack
sifter

CHOCO-WAKKA COOKIES

makes about 4 dozen cookies

INGREDIENTS

- 2 cups plus 2 tablespoons flour
- ¾ cup cocoa powder
- 1 teaspoon baking soda
- ½ teaspoon salt
- 1¼ cups butter, softened
- 2 cups sugar
- 2 eggs
- 1 tablespoon vanilla extract
- 12 ounces (340 g) semisweet chocolate chips

1. Preheat the oven to 350 degrees.
2. Whisk together the flour, cocoa powder, baking soda, and salt. Set this bowl aside.
3. Cream the butter and sugar until it is light and fluffy.
4. Beat in the eggs one at a time. Then beat in the vanilla extract.
5. Stir in the flour mixture and then the chocolate chips.
6. Using dinner spoons, drop the cookie dough onto an ungreased cookie sheet. Space the cookies about 2 inches (5 cm) apart.
7. Bake for 8 to 10 minutes. Let the cookies cool on the pan for about 2 minutes. Then transfer them to the cooling rack with a spatula.

TOOLS & EQUIPMENT

mixing bowls
measuring cups
measuring spoons
whisk
electric mixer
silicone spatula
mixing spoon
dinner spoons
cookie sheets
spatula
cooling rack

APRICOT COOKIES

makes about 24 cookies

INGREDIENTS

- 1 cup butter, softened
- 1 3-ounce (85-g) package cream cheese, softened
- ¼ teaspoon vanilla extract
- ¼ teaspoon salt
- 2 cups all-purpose flour
- 1 cup sugar
- 24 dried apricots

1. Preheat the oven to 350 degrees.
2. Put the butter and cream cheese in a large bowl. Stir until fluffy.
3. Add the vanilla extract, salt, flour, and sugar. Stir well.
4. Make sure the counter is clean and dry. Then sprinkle it with flour. Put the cookie dough on the floured area. Roll out the dough with a rolling pin.
5. Use the cookie cutter to cut out circles of dough. Cut as many as you can out of the dough. You will need to roll out the dough again several times.
6. Put a dried apricot on one of the circles. Put another circle on the top. Press the edges of the dough together around the apricot. Repeat until you've used all of the circles.
7. Arrange the cookies on a baking sheet. Bake for 10 minutes. Take the cookies out of the oven. Let them cool.

TOOLS & EQUIPMENT

large mixing bowl
measuring cups
measuring spoons
mixing spoon
rolling pin
3-inch (7.6-cm) round cookie cutter
baking sheet

SURPRISE MERINGUES

makes about 2 dozen cookies

INGREDIENTS

- 2 egg whites at room temperature
- ⅛ teaspoon cream of tartar
- ½ teaspoon salt
- 1 teaspoon vanilla extract
- ¾ cup sugar
- 1 cup semisweet chocolate chips
- ½ cup chopped walnuts (optional)

1. Preheat the oven to 300 degrees. Line the cookie sheets with parchment paper and set them aside.
2. Put the egg whites, cream of tartar, and salt in a bowl. Whip until soft peaks form. Then beat in the vanilla extract.
3. Continue beating the egg mixture while gradually adding the sugar.
4. Stir in the chocolate chips and the walnuts.
5. Drop spoonfuls of the batter onto the paper-lined cookie sheets. Space them about 2 inches (5 cm) apart.
6. Bake for 25 minutes.
7. Leave the cookies on the paper until they are completely cool. Then carefully peel them from the paper.

TOOLS & EQUIPMENT

cookie sheets
parchment paper
mixing bowls
measuring spoons
electric mixer
silicone spatula
measuring cups
dinner spoons
spatula

CHRISTMAS COCHINITOS

makes about 3 dozen cookies

INGREDIENTS

FOR THE COOKIES

- 2¼ cups flour
- ½ teaspoon baking powder
- ½ teaspoon baking soda
- ¾ cup butter
- ½ cup packed brown sugar
- ½ cup corn syrup
- 1 teaspoon vanilla extract
- zest of 1 orange, finely grated
- 1 teaspoon cinnamon

FOR THE TOPPING

- 2 tablespoons sugar
- 1 teaspoon cinnamon

1. Whisk together the flour, baking powder, and baking soda in a bowl.
2. In a separate bowl, cream the butter until it is light and fluffy. Beat in the brown sugar, corn syrup, vanilla extract, orange zest, and cinnamon.
3. Add the flour mixture in thirds. Stir well after each addition. Form the dough into two balls. Cover them in plastic wrap. Refrigerate them for about 2 hours.

4. Preheat the oven to 375 degrees. Grease the cookie sheets and set them aside.
5. Lightly flour the countertop and place one ball of dough on it. Roll out the dough until it is ¼ inch (0.6 cm) thick. Cut out cookies with a pig-shaped cookie cutter. Place the cookies on a cookie sheet. Gather the scraps and set them aside.
6. Roll out the other ball of dough and cut out more cookies. Combine the scraps from both balls. Roll them out to make more cookies. Keep rolling out the scraps and cutting cookies until all the dough is used.
7. When you are ready to bake the cookies, stir together the sugar and cinnamon to make the topping. Sprinkle a light dusting of cinnamon-sugar over the cookies. Bake for about 10 minutes or until the cookies are light brown. Let the cookies cool on the cookie sheet for about 3 minutes. Then use a spatula to move them to a cooling rack.

TOOLS & EQUIPMENT

- measuring cups
- measuring spoons
- mixing bowls
- whisk
- electric mixer
- zester or grater
- silicone spatula
- plastic wrap
- cookie sheets
- rolling pin
- pig-shaped cookie cutter
- cooling rack
- spatula

BODACIOUS BROWNIES

makes 9 brownies

INGREDIENTS

6 ounces (170 g) bittersweet chocolate (not unsweetened)
½ cup butter
2 eggs
1 cup sugar
1 tablespoon cocoa powder
1 teaspoon vanilla extract
1 teaspoon cinnamon
½ teaspoon salt
1 cup flour

TOOLS & EQUIPMENT

8 × 8-inch baking pan
aluminum foil
measuring cups
saucepan
mixing spoon
mixing bowl
measuring spoons
silicone spatula
toothpick
cooling rack
knife

1. Preheat the oven to 350 degrees. Line the baking pan with aluminum foil. Grease the foil. Set the pan aside.
2. Put the chocolate and the butter in the saucepan. Heat, stirring often, on medium-low until the butter and chocolate are melted. Remove the pan from the heat. Let the mixture cool to room temperature.
3. Put the chocolate mixture in a mixing bowl. Add the eggs, sugar, cocoa powder, vanilla extract, cinnamon, and salt. Stir just until mixed.
4. Stir in the flour.
5. Pour the batter into the prepared pan. Use a silicone spatula to spread the batter evenly. Bake for about 25 to 30 minutes. It's done when a toothpick stuck in the center comes out clean. Place the pan on a cooling rack until the brownies cool completely.
6. Use the edges of the foil to lift the brownies from the pan. Cut them into squares.

TERRIFIC TURTLE BARS

makes about 32 bars

INGREDIENTS

FOR THE CRUST LAYER

- 2 cups flour
- 1 cup packed brown sugar
- ½ cup plus 2 tablespoons butter, softened
- 1½ cups pecan halves

FOR THE CARAMEL LAYER

- ⅔ cup butter
- ½ cup packed brown sugar

FOR THE TOPPING

- 12 ounces (340 g) semisweet chocolate chips

TOOLS & EQUIPMENT

- mixing bowl
- measuring cups
- mixing spoon
- pastry blender
- 9 × 13-inch baking dish
- saucepan
- silicone spatula
- cooling rack
- knife

1. Preheat the oven to 350 degrees.
2. Stir together the flour and the brown sugar. Cut in the butter until the mixture resembles fine crumbs.
3. Pour this mixture into the baking dish. Pat it down evenly.
4. Sprinkle the pecan halves evenly over the crust.
5. Now make the caramel layer. Put the butter and the brown sugar in the saucepan. Cook over medium heat, stirring constantly, until the entire surface bubbles.
6. Have an adult helper pour the hot caramel over the pecans.
7. Bake for 18 to 22 minutes. The entire surface of the caramel should be bubbling.
8. Place the pan on a cooling rack. After 5 minutes, sprinkle the chocolate chips over the caramel layer. When the chocolate has melted, spread it over the entire surface. Cool completely before cutting the bars.

SWEET S'MORES BARS

makes 16 bars

- 6 tablespoons butter
- ¼ cup brown sugar
- 6 tablespoons maple syrup
- 2 cups rolled oats
- ½ cup flour
- ¼ teaspoon salt
- 1 cup graham cracker crumbs
- ½ teaspoon cinnamon
- 1½ cups chocolate chips
- 1½ cups mini marshmallows

TOOLS & EQUIPMENT

- 8 × 8-inch baking pan
- parchment paper
- saucepan
- measuring cups
- measuring spoons
- mixing spoon
- silicone spatula
- microwave-safe bowl

1. Preheat the oven to 350 degrees. Line the pan with the parchment paper.
2. Have an adult help melt the butter in a saucepan over medium-low heat. Add the brown sugar and syrup. Stir and cook about 5 minutes or until the sugar dissolves. Take the saucepan off the heat.
3. Add the oats, flour, salt, graham cracker crumbs, cinnamon, and 1 cup chocolate chips to the saucepan. Stir well. Press the mixture into the baking pan.
4. Bake for 15 minutes. Take the pan out of the oven. Add the marshmallows in an even layer. Bake for 5 minutes. Let the bars cool.
5. Put the remaining chocolate chips in a microwave-safe bowl. Microwave for 30 seconds. Stir. Repeat until the chips are melted. Drizzle the chocolate over the bars. Chill the bars for 1 hour.

PIES & TARTS

You can use almost any fresh fruit to make a pie or tart. Popular choices include apples, pears, peaches, nectarines, rhubarb, strawberries, blueberries, and cherries. The main difference between a pie and tart is in the pans that you use. Pie pans have sloped sides and tart pans have vertical sides. Plus, the bottom of a tart pan can be removed. So, tarts look fancier because you can serve them on pretty platters. Pies are always served in the pans you make them in.

Scrumptious Fruit Tart

Pretty as a Pecan Pie

French Silk Pie
Glorious Ginger
Pear Tart
Mighty Mixed
Fruit Pie

BASIC PIE & TART SHELLS

makes 1 pie or tart shell

INGREDIENTS

2 cups all-purpose flour
¼ cup sugar
½ teaspoon salt
12 tablespoons (1½ sticks) butter, cut into ½-inch (1.3-cm) cubes and chilled
4 to 6 tablespoons ice water

TOOLS & EQUIPMENT

mixing bowl
measuring cups
measuring spoons
whisk
knife
cutting board
silicone spatula
pastry blender
fork
plastic wrap
rolling pin
tape measure or ruler
9-inch pie pan or tart pan
parchment paper or waxed paper
pie weights or dried beans

TO MAKE THE DOUGH

1. Whisk together the flour, sugar, and salt in a mixing bowl. Stir in the butter cubes.
2. Use the pastry blender to cut the butter into the flour mixture. Work quickly while the butter is still cold. Stop when the pieces of butter are pea-sized and smaller.
3. Add the ice water a little bit at a time. Use a fork to mix it in. Stop adding water when you can form the dough into a ball.
4. Divide the dough into two equal parts. Shape them into discs and wrap each one in plastic wrap. Put the discs of dough in the refrigerator for 30 minutes.
5. Sprinkle a light layer of flour on the countertop. Unwrap one disc of dough and place it on the flour. Press down evenly with your hands to flatten the disc some more.
6. Roll out the crust. Start with the rolling pin in the middle. Roll out toward the edge. Put the rolling pin in the middle again. Roll in the opposite direction from last time.
7. Gently lift the dough and turn it over. Begin rolling again. Change directions often as you roll out the dough. Otherwise, you will get

an oval instead of a circle! Continue rolling in all directions until the dough is 11 inches (28 cm) across.

8. If your recipe calls for a top crust, you will need the second disc of dough. First, fill the pie according to the recipe. Then turn back to these pages and repeat steps 5 through 7 to make the top crust. If your recipe doesn't call for a top crust, you can freeze the extra dough to use later.

FOR AN UNBAKED PIE SHELL

1. Set the rolling pin at one edge of the dough. Lift the edge of the dough and gently roll the dough onto the pin. When you reach the center, carefully pick up the rolling pin and dough. Position it over the pie pan. Unroll the pie dough onto the pie pan.

2. Gently press the dough into the pan. It should touch the pan all over. If the dough tears, pinch it back together. Using a knife, trim the dough about ½ inch (1.3 cm) beyond the edge of the pan. Use the scraps to patch any holes in the crust.
3. Lift the edge of the crust and tuck the excess dough under to make a thick edge. Crimp the edge with your fingertips or a fork.

FOR AN UNBAKED TART SHELL

1. Place the rolled-out dough over the tart pan. Be careful not to tear it on the edges of the pan.

A REAL TIMESAVER

If you're pressed for time, use a frozen piecrust. They come already rolled out or ready to roll. Often, they're just as good as homemade. And, professional food stylists swear by them! You can still make the filling and use your own pie pan.

2. Gently press the dough against the bottom and sides. Work slowly and carefully. Don't cut yourself on the edges of the pan.
3. Trim the excess dough by rolling the rolling pin over the pan.

FOR A BLIND-BAKED PIE OR TART SHELL

1. Preheat the oven to 375 degrees.
2. Make an unbaked pie or tart shell.
3. Place a piece of parchment paper or waxed paper in the crust. Gently flatten it against the crust. Cover the paper evenly with pie weights or dried beans. This will keep the crust from rising and bubbling while it bakes.

4. Bake the crust for about 20 minutes. It should be lightly browned. Remove the pan from the oven. Carefully remove the pie weights and paper. Ask an adult to help you do this! Prick the bottom of the crust with a fork about five times. Put the crust back in the oven for another 5 minutes. Cool the crust completely before filling it.

AMAZING APPLE PIE

makes 8 servings

INGREDIENTS

½ cup sugar
1 teaspoon cinnamon
¼ teaspoon nutmeg
¼ teaspoon salt
1 tablespoon tapioca flakes or cornstarch
8 apples
9-inch (23-cm) unbaked pie shell and top crust (see pp. 100–103)
ice cream (optional)

TOOLS & EQUIPMENT

mixing bowls
measuring cups
measuring spoons
whisk
vegetable peeler
apple slicer and corer
knife
cutting board
9-inch pie pan
silicone spatula
fork
old cookie sheet
cooling rack

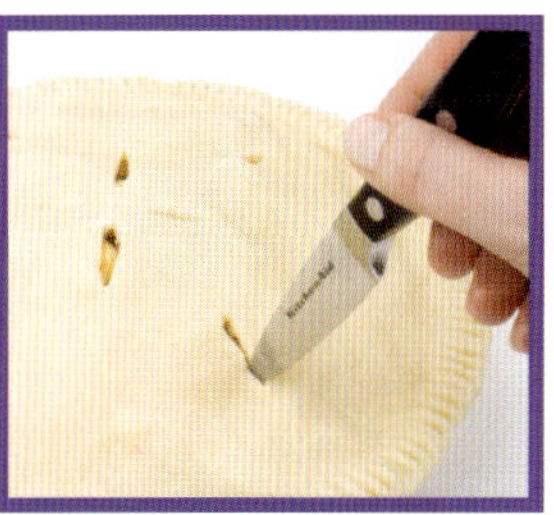

1. Preheat the oven to 400 degrees. In a small mixing bowl, whisk together the sugar, cinnamon, nutmeg, salt, and tapioca. Set this bowl aside.
2. Peel the apples. Slice them with the apple slicer and corer. Cut each slice in half lengthwise to make thinner slices.
3. Put the apple slices in a mixing bowl. Pour the sugar mixture over them. Stir gently to evenly coat the slices with the sugar mixture.
4. Pour the apple slices into the pie shell. The apples should stick above the crust. The apples will settle and shrink as the pie bakes and cools.
5. Place the top crust over the filled pie shell. Remove any dough overhanging the edge of the pan. Crimp the edges of the crust with your fingertips or a fork. Cut several small slits in the top crust with a knife. These vents will allow steam to escape while the pie bakes.
6. Bake the pie for 30 to 40 minutes. Put an old cookie sheet on the rack below the pie pan. This will catch any juice that bubbles out of the pie.
7. Cool the pie on a cooling rack. Serve the pie when it is still warm. Try adding a scoop of ice cream on top!

THE BEST PIE APPLES

Cortland (tart)
Granny Smith (tart)
Jonathan (tart)
Pippin (tart)
Winesap (tart)
McIntosh (sweet-tart)
Gala (sweet)
Empire (sweet)
Fuji (sweet)
Pink Lady (sweet)

PRETTY AS A PECAN PIE

makes 8 servings

INGREDIENTS

- 9-inch (23-cm) unbaked pie shell (see pp. 100–103)
- 1½ cups pecan halves
- 1 cup light corn syrup
- 3 eggs
- 1 cup sugar
- ½ teaspoon salt
- 2 tablespoons butter, melted
- 1 teaspoon vanilla extract
- ice cream (optional)

1. Preheat the oven to 350 degrees.
2. Spread the pecans in the pie shell. Set it aside.
3. In a mixing bowl, stir together the corn syrup, eggs, sugar, salt, butter, and vanilla extract. Pour the mixture over the pecans.
4. Bake for 50 to 60 minutes. Lightly tap the pie's center to test for doneness. It will spring back when the pie is done.
5. Cool the pie on a cooling rack. Try serving the pie with ice cream!

TOOLS & EQUIPMENT

9-inch pie pan
mixing bowl
measuring cups
measuring spoons
silicone spatula
cooling rack

FRENCH SILK PIE

makes 8 servings

INGREDIENTS

FOR THE SHELL

about 30 vanilla wafers (enough to make 2 cups of crumbs)

¼ cup butter, melted

FOR THE FILLING

3 1-ounce (28-g) squares unsweetened chocolate

1 cup butter, softened

2 cups powdered sugar

4 pasteurized eggs

2 teaspoons vanilla extract

chocolate shavings (optional)

TOOLS & EQUIPMENT

gallon-size zipper bag

rolling pin

measuring cup

mixing bowls

fork

9-inch pie pan

double boiler or microwave oven

electric mixer

silicone spatula

1. Put the vanilla wafers in the zipper bag and close it. Roll over the bag with a rolling pin to crush the wafers into crumbs. The crumbs should be fine but not powdery.
2. Put the crumbs in the mixing bowl and add the melted butter. Stir with a fork until they are well mixed.
3. Pour the crumb mixture into the pie pan. Press the crumb mixture evenly and firmly into the bottom and up the sides of the pan.
4. The crust is done! Refrigerate the crust while you make the filling.
5. Melt the chocolate in a double boiler or a microwave oven. Let it cool to room temperature.
6. Cream the butter and sugar until it is light and fluffy. If you have a stand mixer, use it. It will make the next step easier. Beat in the cooled, melted chocolate.
7. Add the eggs one at a time. Beat the mixture for 5 minutes after you add each egg. Really, 5 minutes per egg! Scrape down the sides of the bowl every few minutes.
8. Stir in the vanilla extract.
9. Spoon the mixture into the prepared pie shell. Chill the pie for several hours. Try serving each slice with a chocolate shaving on top!

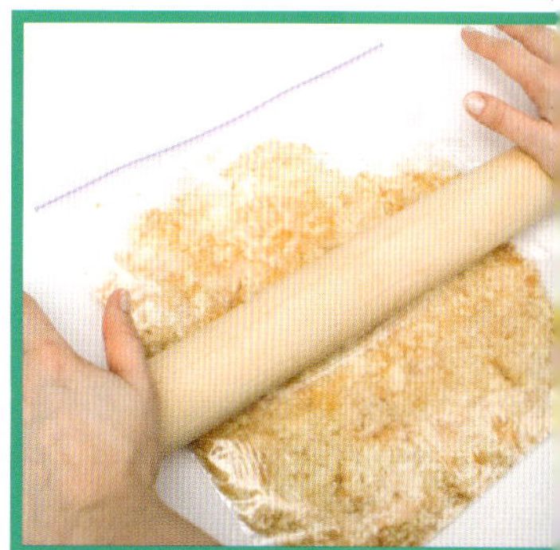

MIGHTY MIXED FRUIT PIE

makes 8 servings

INGREDIENTS

- non-stick cooking spray
- 9-inch (23-cm) premade piecrust
- 1 pear, diced
- 1 apple, diced
- 4 tablespoons brown sugar
- 1½ teaspoons vanilla extract
- 2 tablespoons lemon juice
- ¼ teaspoon salt
- ¼ cup dried blueberries

1. Preheat the oven to 350 degrees. Grease the pie plate with non-stick cooking spray.
2. Press the premade piecrust into the pie plate.
3. Bake for 25 minutes, or until golden brown. Remove the pie plate from the oven. Set aside to cool.
4. Heat the pear, apple, brown sugar, vanilla extract, lemon juice, and salt in a large saucepan over low heat. Stir often. Cook for 30 to 40 minutes, or until the fruit is soft. Add the blueberries. Cook for 5 more minutes. Remove saucepan from heat. Let it cool.
5. Pour the cooled fruit mixture into the cooled crust.
6. Sprinkle some brown sugar on top and bake for 25 minutes. Remove it from the oven. Let it cool before serving.

TOOLS & EQUIPMENT

pie plate
knife
cutting board
measuring spoons
large saucepan
mixing spoon
measuring cups

RHUBARB BERRY PIE

makes 8 servings

INGREDIENTS

- non-stick cooking spray
- 9-inch (23-cm) premade piecrust
- 1 cup sugar
- 1¼ cup flour
- 3 cups chopped rhubarb
- 3 cups chopped strawberries
- 1 cup brown sugar
- ¼ cup butter
- ½ teaspoon cinnamon

1. Preheat the oven to 425 degrees. Grease the pie plate with non-stick cooking spray. Place the piecrust in the pie plate.
2. Put the sugar and ¼ cup flour in a large mixing bowl. Stir. Add the rhubarb and berries. Stir to coat the rhubarb and berries. Let it sit 30 minutes. Pour the rhubarb mixture into the pie plate.
3. Put the brown sugar, butter, cinnamon, and 1 cup flour in a medium bowl. Stir until the mixture is crumbly.
4. Sprinkle mixture evenly over the pie filling. Cover the pie with aluminum foil. Bake for 15 minutes. Take the pie out of the oven. Turn the oven down to 375 degrees.
5. Remove the aluminum foil from the pie. Bake for 35 minutes or until the top is golden brown. Let the pie cool.

TOOLS & EQUIPMENT

pie plate
measuring cups
mixing bowls
mixing spoons
knife
cutting board
measuring spoons
aluminum foil

OH MY, CHICKEN PIE

makes 8 servings

INGREDIENTS

- 1 pound (0.45 kg) skinless, boneless chicken
- 1 cup sliced carrots
- ½ cup green peas
- ½ cup sliced celery
- 3 small red potatoes, cubed
- 5 cups chicken broth
- ⅓ cup chopped onion
- ⅓ cup butter
- ⅓ cup flour
- ½ teaspoon salt
- ¼ teaspoon black pepper
- ½ teaspoon garlic salt
- 1 cup milk
- 2 9-inch (23-cm) premade piecrusts

1. Ask an adult for help. Preheat the oven to 425 degrees. Put the chicken, carrots, peas, celery, and potatoes in a medium saucepan. Add 3 cups chicken broth. Stir. Boil for 15 minutes. Remove from heat. Drain the mixture.

2. In another saucepan, cook the onion and butter over medium heat for 10 minutes. Add the flour, salt, pepper, and garlic salt.
3. Slowly stir the milk and remaining chicken broth into the onion mixture. Simmer over medium heat for 5 minutes, or until the mixture is thick. Remove from heat.

4. Lay one piecrust in the pie plate. Add the chicken mixture. Spread it out evenly. Pour the onion mixture over the chicken mixture.
5. Lay the second piecrust over the top. Use a fork to press the edges of the crusts together. Make four small cuts in the top crust.

6. Bake 35 minutes or until the top is golden brown. Remove it from the oven. Let cool for 10 minutes.

TOOLS & EQUIPMENT

knife
cutting board
measuring cups
saucepans
mixing spoon
colander
measuring spoons
pie plate
fork

SCRUMPTIOUS FRUIT TART

makes 8 servings

INGREDIENTS

- 2 eggs
- ½ cup sugar
- ½ cup lemon juice (from 2 to 3 lemons)
- 4 tablespoons butter, cut into pieces
- 9-inch (23-cm) blind-baked tart shell (see pp. 100–103)
- 2 cups of fresh fruit such as blueberries, strawberries, peaches, kiwifruit, or raspberries

1. Put some water in the bottom of the double boiler. Insert the top pan and turn the heat to low. Put the eggs and the sugar in the top pan. Whisk them together.
2. Add the lemon juice and the butter. Continue stirring the mixture until it thickens, about 10 minutes. You just made lemon curd! Remove it from the heat and cool it in the refrigerator.
3. Prepare the fruit. Slice large fruits such as kiwifruit or peaches. Cut strawberries in half. Leave small berries whole. Decide how you want to arrange the fruit. You can use just one type of fruit or a few.
4. Pour the cooled lemon curd into the tart shell. Spread it evenly with a silicone spatula.
5. Arrange the fruit on top of the lemon curd. If you aren't serving the tart right away, put it in the refrigerator.

TOOLS & EQUIPMENT

double boiler
measuring cups
whisk
juicer
knife
cutting board
9-inch tart pan
silicone spatula

IN A RUSH?

You can buy ready-made lemon curd at many grocery stores. You can also use instant custard instead of lemon curd. Just follow the directions on the package. Lemon or vanilla custard works well for fruit tarts.

GLORIOUS GINGER PEAR TART

makes 8 servings

INGREDIENTS

- 3 to 4 ripe pears
- 3 tablespoons butter
- 3 tablespoons sugar
- 1 tablespoon water
- ¼ cup chopped crystallized ginger
- 9-inch (23-cm) tart shell, unbaked and chilled (see pp. 100–103)

TOOLS & EQUIPMENT

- vegetable peeler
- knife
- cutting board
- spoon
- measuring cups
- measuring spoons
- saucepan
- silicone spatula
- mixing bowl
- 9-inch tart pan
- cooling rack

1. Preheat the oven to 375 degrees.
2. Peel the pears and cut them in half lengthwise. Use the spoon to scoop out the cores. Cut each pear half into lengthwise slices about ½ inch (1.3 cm) thick.
3. Put the butter, sugar, water, and ginger in a small saucepan. Simmer the mixture over medium heat until the sugar dissolves. Stir the mixture often.
4. Put the pear slices in a mixing bowl. Pour the sugar mixture over the pears. Stir gently to coat the pears.
5. Pour the pear mixture into the prepared tart shell. If you like, arrange the pears in a pretty pattern.
6. Bake the tart for about 35 to 40 minutes. Cool it on a cooling rack.

TRY THIS

Baking a filled tart on a pizza stone helps crisp the crust. Cover the pizza stone with aluminum foil. Set it and the tart on the middle rack. If you don't have a pizza stone, no worries. The tart will bake fine without it too.

MUFFINS & QUICK BREADS

Muffins and quick breads start as batters that are stirred and poured into pans to bake. A batter is a mix of wet and dry ingredients that is thin enough to be poured. Muffins and quick breads are made with baking soda or baking powder instead of yeast. That means you can bake the bread as soon as you mix the batter.

Savory Herb Pull-Aparts

Sweet Cinnamon Muffins

Sweet Blueberry Muffins

Ideal Poppy Seed Muffins
Fruity Flavorful Bread
Supreme Gran-Apple Snack
Zesty Zucchini Bread

SWEET BLUEBERRY MUFFINS

makes 12 muffins

INGREDIENTS

- ¾ cup whole milk
- ¼ cup vegetable oil
- 2 eggs
- 1 teaspoon vanilla extract
- ¾ cup all-purpose flour
- ¾ cup whole wheat flour
- 2 teaspoons baking powder
- ¼ teaspoon salt
- ⅔ cup and 1 tablespoon sugar
- 2 cups blueberries

1. Preheat the oven to 375 degrees. Put paper liners in the muffin tin.
2. In a small mixing bowl, whisk together the milk, oil, eggs, and vanilla extract. Set this bowl aside.
3. Put the flour, baking powder, salt, and ⅔ cup sugar in a large bowl. Stir.
4. Add the milk mixture to the flour mixture. Stir with a silicone spatula. Add the blueberries. Stir lightly.
5. Divide the batter evenly between the paper liners.
6. Sprinkle the remaining sugar on top of the muffins.
7. Bake 20 minutes or until golden brown. Let the muffins cool.

TOOLS & EQUIPMENT

paper liners
muffin tin
mixing bowls
measuring cups
measuring spoons
whisk
mixing spoon
silicone spatula
scoop

MARVELOUS MORNING MUFFINS

makes 12 muffins

INGREDIENTS

- 2 to 3 large carrots, peeled
- 1 apple, peeled and cored
- 2 cups whole wheat flour
- 1 cup brown sugar
- 2 teaspoons baking soda
- 2 teaspoons cinnamon
- ⅓ teaspoon salt
- ¼ cup flaked coconut
- ½ cup chopped walnuts
- 3 eggs
- ⅔ cup vegetable oil
- 2 teaspoons vanilla extract
- ¼ cup orange juice
- ½ cup raisins
- ¼ cup old fashioned oats

1. Preheat the oven to 375 degrees. Put paper liners in the muffin tin and set it aside. Grate the carrots and apple and set them aside.
2. Put the flour, sugar, baking soda, cinnamon, and salt in a large mixing bowl. Stir.
3. Stir in the grated apple, coconut, walnuts, and 2 cups grated carrots.
4. Put the eggs, oil, vanilla extract, and orange juice in a small bowl. Stir. Add the egg mixture to the flour mixture. Stir and then stir in the raisins.

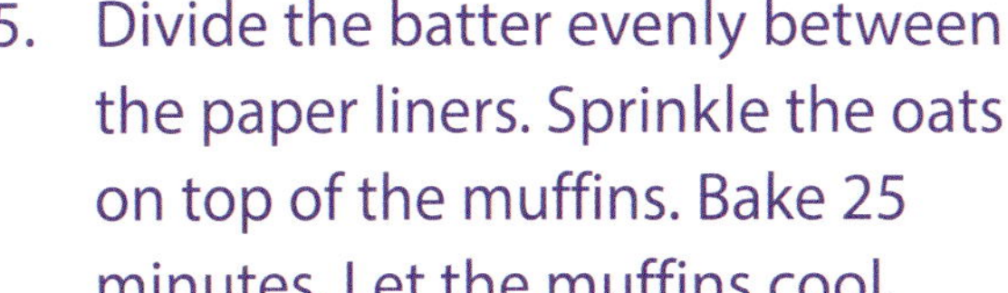

5. Divide the batter evenly between the paper liners. Sprinkle the oats on top of the muffins. Bake 25 minutes. Let the muffins cool.

TOOLS & EQUIPMENT

paper liners
muffin tin
peeler
apple peeler and corer
grater
mixing bowls
measuring cups
measuring spoons
mixing spoon
knife
cutting board
scoop

TASTY OAT & RAISIN SURPRISE

makes 12 muffins

INGREDIENTS

- non-stick cooking spray
- ¾ cup whole milk
- ½ cup applesauce
- ¾ cup raisins
- 1 egg
- 1 teaspoon vanilla extract
- 1 cup whole wheat flour
- ¾ cup rolled oats
- ⅓ cup brown sugar
- 3 teaspoons baking powder
- ½ teaspoon salt
- 1 teaspoon cinnamon
- ⅛ teaspoon ground cloves

1. Preheat the oven to 400 degrees. Grease the muffin tin with non-stick cooking spray.
2. Put the milk, applesauce, raisins, egg, and vanilla extract in a small mixing bowl. Stir with a silicone spatula.
3. Put the flour, oats, sugar, baking powder, salt, cinnamon, and ground cloves in a large bowl. Stir with a silicone spatula.
4. Add the milk mixture to the flour mixture. Stir.
5. Divide the batter evenly between the muffin cups. Bake 15 minutes or until golden brown. Let the muffins cool.

TOOLS & EQUIPMENT

muffin tin
mixing bowls
measuring cups
measuring spoons
silicone spatula
scoop

ZUCCHINI COCOA-NUT NIBBLES

makes 12 muffins

INGREDIENTS

- 1 zucchini
- 1 egg
- 1 teaspoon vanilla extract
- ⅔ cup sugar
- ⅓ cup vegetable oil
- 1¼ teaspoon baking soda
- ¼ teaspoon salt
- 1½ cups all-purpose flour
- ½ teaspoon cinnamon
- 1 tablespoon unsweetened cocoa powder
- 1 cup chopped walnuts

1. Preheat the oven to 350 degrees. Put paper liners in the muffin tin.
2. Grate the zucchini onto a paper towel. Gently squeeze the towel around the zucchini to remove extra water. Put the zucchini in a 2-cup measuring cup. Press it into the cup. Stop when you have 1½ cups of zucchini.
3. In a medium mixing bowl, whisk together the egg and vanilla extract. Stir in the zucchini, sugar, and oil. Stir in the baking soda and salt.
4. Put the flour, cinnamon, and cocoa powder in a small bowl. Stir. Add the zucchini mixture to the flour mixture. Stir and then stir in the chopped walnuts.
5. Divide the batter evenly between the paper liners. Bake 30 minutes. Let the muffins cool.

TOOLS & EQUIPMENT

paper liners
muffin tin
grater
paper towel
measuring cups
mixing bowls
measuring spoons
whisk
mixing spoon
scoop

SUPREME GRAN-APPLE SNACK

makes 16 muffins

INGREDIENTS

- non-stick cooking spray
- 5 medium apples
- ½ cup brown sugar
- 2 eggs
- 8 tablespoons unsalted butter, softened
- 2 teaspoons vanilla extract
- 1⅓ cups granola
- 2 cups whole wheat flour
- 1 teaspoon baking powder
- ½ teaspoon baking soda
- 1 teaspoon cinnamon
- ½ teaspoon nutmeg
- ½ teaspoon salt

1. Preheat the oven to 325 degrees. Grease the muffin tins with non-stick cooking spray and set them aside.
2. Core and peel the apples. Cut them into thin slices. Dice all but 16 of the slices.
3. Put the brown sugar and 3½ cups diced apples in a large mixing bowl. Stir.
4. In a medium bowl, whisk together the eggs, butter, and vanilla extract. Add the egg mixture to the apple mixture. Stir in the granola.
5. In a small bowl, whisk together the flour, baking powder, baking soda, cinnamon, nutmeg, and salt. Slowly stir the flour mixture into the apple mixture.
6. Divide the batter evenly between 16 muffin cups. Fill the cups to the top. Place an apple slice on top of each filled cup. Bake 25 minutes. Let the muffins cool.

TOOLS & EQUIPMENT

2 muffin tins
apple peeler and corer
knife
cutting board
mixing bowls
measuring cups
mixing spoon
measuring spoons
whisk
scoop

SWEET CINNAMON MUFFINS

makes 24 muffins

INGREDIENTS

FOR THE MUFFINS

non-stick cooking spray
2½ cups all-purpose flour
1½ teaspoons baking powder
½ teaspoon baking soda
¼ teaspoon salt
10 tablespoons unsalted butter, softened
1 cup sugar
3 eggs
1½ teaspoons vanilla extract
1¼ cups sour cream

FOR THE TOPPING

2¼ cups all-purpose flour
¾ cup brown sugar
2 teaspoons cinnamon
½ teaspoon salt
10 tablespoons unsalted butter, softened
2 cups powdered sugar
¼ cup whole milk

1. Preheat the oven to 350 degrees. Grease the muffin tins with non-stick cooking spray. In a large mixing bowl, whisk together the flour, baking powder, baking soda, and salt.
2. In a medium bowl, whisk together the butter and sugar. Whisk in the eggs and vanilla extract. Add the butter mixture to the flour mixture. Stir with a silicone spatula. Stir in the sour cream. Divide the batter evenly between the muffin cups.
3. Make the topping. Put the flour, brown sugar, cinnamon, salt, and butter in a medium bowl. Stir. Sprinkle the topping on the muffins. Bake 25 minutes. Let cool 10 minutes.
4. In a small bowl, whisk together the powdered sugar and milk. Drizzle it over the muffins with a spoon.

TOOLS & EQUIPMENT

2 muffin tins
mixing bowls
measuring cups
measuring spoons
whisk
silicone spatula
scoop
spoon

DREAMY CHOCOLATY MUFFINS

makes 12 muffins

INGREDIENTS

- 1⅛ cups all-purpose flour
- ½ cup unsweetened cocoa powder
- ¾ teaspoon baking soda
- ¼ teaspoon salt
- ½ cup sugar
- 1 cup semisweet chocolate chips
- ½ cup unsalted butter, softened
- 2 eggs
- ½ cup yogurt
- ¼ cup whole milk
- ¼ cup vegetable oil
- ½ teaspoon vanilla extract

1. Preheat the oven to 325 degrees. Put paper liners in the muffin tin and set it aside.
2. Put the flour, cocoa powder, baking soda, salt, sugar, and chocolate chips in a large mixing bowl. Stir.
3. In a medium bowl, whisk together the butter, eggs, yogurt, milk, oil, and vanilla extract.
4. Add the butter mixture to the flour mixture. Stir.
5. Fill the paper liners two-thirds full of batter. Bake 17 minutes. Let the muffins cool.

TOOLS & EQUIPMENT

paper liners
muffin tin
mixing bowls
measuring cups
measuring spoons
mixing spoon
whisk
scoop

IDEAL POPPY SEED MUFFINS

makes 12 muffins

INGREDIENTS

- 2 lemons
- 2 cups all-purpose flour
- 1 cup sugar
- 2 teaspoons baking powder
- ¼ teaspoon baking soda
- ¼ teaspoon salt
- ¾ cup sour cream
- 2 eggs
- 1¼ teaspoons vanilla extract
- ½ cup unsalted butter, softened
- 2 tablespoons poppy seeds

1. Preheat the oven to 400 degrees. Put paper liners in the muffin tin.
2. Zest the lemons into a large mixing bowl. Add the flour, sugar, baking powder, baking soda, and salt. Stir.
3. Put the sour cream, eggs, vanilla extract, and butter in a medium bowl. Stir.
4. Cut the lemons in half. Squeeze the juice into the sour cream mixture. Remove any seeds. Whisk until smooth.
5. Add the sour cream mixture to the flour mixture. Whisk in the poppy seeds.
6. Divide the batter evenly between the paper liners. Bake 18 minutes or until the tops look golden. Let the muffins cool.

TOOLS & EQUIPMENT

paper liners
muffin tin
zester or grater
mixing bowls
measuring cups
measuring spoons
mixing spoon
knife
cutting board
whisk
scoop

SWEET STRAWBERRIES & CREAM

makes 12 muffins

INGREDIENTS

non-stick cooking spray
4 ounces (113 g) cream cheese
3 eggs
2 teaspoons vanilla extract
2 cups all-purpose flour
¾ cup sugar
2½ teaspoons baking powder
½ teaspoon salt
½ cup unsalted butter, softened
1 cup whole milk
1 cup chopped strawberries
⅓ cup brown sugar

1. Preheat the oven to 400 degrees. Grease the muffin tin with non-stick cooking spray.
2. Put the cream cheese, 1 egg, and 1¼ teaspoons vanilla extract in a small mixing bowl. Stir.
3. In a large bowl, whisk together the flour, sugar, baking powder, and salt.
4. In a medium bowl, whisk together the butter, milk, 2 eggs, and remaining vanilla extract. Add the butter mixture to the flour mixture. Stir.
5. Fill each muffin cup halfway with batter. Add a layer of strawberries in each cup.
6. Add a teaspoon of the cream cheese mixture to each muffin cup. Then add 2 tablespoons of muffin batter to each muffin cup. Sprinkle extra strawberries and the brown sugar on top of the muffins. Bake 15 minutes. Let the muffins cool.

TOOLS & EQUIPMENT

- muffin tin
- measuring spoons
- mixing bowls
- mixing spoon
- measuring cups
- whisk
- scoop
- knife
- cutting board

MINI PANCAKE MUFFINS

makes 24 muffins

INGREDIENTS

- non-stick cooking spray
- 1 cup all-purpose flour
- 1 teaspoon baking powder
- ½ teaspoon baking soda
- ¼ teaspoon salt
- 2 tablespoons sugar
- ⅔ cup plain yogurt
- 1 egg
- 2 tablespoons maple syrup
- ¼ teaspoon vanilla extract
- 2 tablespoons unsalted butter, softened
- ½ cup mini chocolate chips

TOOLS & EQUIPMENT

- mini muffin tin
- mixing bowls
- measuring cups
- measuring spoons
- whisk
- mixing spoon
- silicone spatula
- scoop

1. Preheat the oven to 350 degrees. Grease the muffin tin with non-stick cooking spray.
2. In a large mixing bowl, whisk together the flour, baking powder, baking soda, salt, and sugar.
3. Put the yogurt, egg, maple syrup, vanilla extract, and butter in a medium bowl. Stir.
4. Add the yogurt mixture to the flour mixture. Stir with a silicone spatula. The batter should be slightly lumpy.
5. Gently stir in the chocolate chips. Fill the muffin cups two-thirds full of batter. Bake 9 minutes or until golden brown. Let the muffins cool 5 minutes. Serve with maple syrup for dipping.

TRY THIS

Sweeten it up! Add more chocolate or peanut butter chips to the batter before baking.

BANANA CHOCOLATE DELIGHT

makes 18 muffins

INGREDIENTS

- 2 ripe bananas
- ½ cup unsalted butter, softened
- 1¼ cups sugar
- 2 eggs
- 1 teaspoon vanilla extract
- 1½ cups all-purpose flour
- 1 teaspoon baking soda
- ½ teaspoon cinnamon
- ¼ teaspoon salt
- ¾ cup mini chocolate chips

1. Preheat the oven to 350 degrees. Put 9 paper liners in each muffin tin.
2. Put the bananas in a medium mixing bowl. Mash them with a fork.
3. Add the butter, sugar, eggs, and vanilla extract. Stir.
4. In a large bowl, whisk together the flour, baking soda, cinnamon, and salt.
5. Add the banana mixture to the flour mixture. Stir. Add the chocolate chips. Stir just enough to mix them in.
6. Divide the batter evenly between the 18 paper liners. Bake 25 minutes or until golden brown. Let the muffins cool.

TOOLS & EQUIPMENT

paper liners
2 muffin tins
mixing bowls
fork
measuring cups
measuring spoons
silicone spatula
whisk
scoop

PERFECT CIDER DONUT POPS

makes 24 muffins

INGREDIENTS

FOR THE MUFFINS

non-stick cooking spray

¼ cup unsalted butter, softened

½ cup sugar

⅓ cup brown sugar

¼ cup applesauce

3 tablespoons apple juice concentrate, thawed

2 eggs

1 teaspoon vanilla extract

1 cup whole milk

2⅔ cups all-purpose flour

1½ teaspoons baking powder

¼ teaspoon baking soda

¼ teaspoon nutmeg

1 teaspoon cinnamon

¾ teaspoon salt

FOR THE TOPPING

¼ cup unsalted butter

1 teaspoon cinnamon

½ cup sugar

TOOLS & EQUIPMENT

mini muffin tin

mixing bowls

whisk

measuring cups

measuring spoons

silicone spatula

scoop

small microwave-safe bowl

1. Preheat the oven to 375 degrees. Grease the muffin tin with non-stick cooking spray.
2. In a large mixing bowl, whisk together the butter, sugars, applesauce, and apple juice concentrate. Whisk in the eggs, vanilla extract, and milk.
3. In a medium bowl, whisk together the flour, baking powder, baking soda, nutmeg, cinnamon, and salt. Slowly add the flour mixture to the butter mixture. Stir with a silicone spatula.
4. Fill the muffin cups three-fourths full of batter. Bake 15 minutes or until golden brown. Let the muffins cool 5 minutes.
5. Make the topping. Put the butter in a microwave-safe bowl and melt it in the microwave. Put the cinnamon and sugar in a separate bowl. Stir. Dip the top of each muffin in the butter and then in the sugar mixture.

SPICY PUMPKIN POPPERS

makes 24 muffins

INGREDIENTS

FOR THE MUFFINS

non-stick cooking spray
1 cup all-purpose flour
¼ cup sugar
¼ cup brown sugar
2 teaspoons baking powder
1½ teaspoons cinnamon
¼ teaspoon ground ginger
½ teaspoon nutmeg
½ teaspoon salt
1¼ cups pumpkin puree
¼ cup unsalted butter, softened
½ cup evaporated milk
1 egg
1½ teaspoons vanilla extract

FOR THE TOPPING

2 tablespoons sugar
1 teaspoon cinnamon
¼ teaspoon nutmeg

1. Preheat the oven to 400 degrees. Grease the muffin tin with non-stick cooking spray.
2. Put the flour, sugars, baking powder, cinnamon, ginger, nutmeg, and salt in a large mixing bowl. Stir.
3. Put the pumpkin, butter, milk, egg, and vanilla extract in a medium bowl. Stir with a silicone spatula. Add the pumpkin mixture to the flour mixture. Stir.
4. Fill the muffin cups halfway with batter.
5. Put the topping ingredients in a small bowl. Stir. Sprinkle the topping on top of the muffins. Bake 9 minutes. Let the muffins cool.

TRY THIS

Try topping these muffins with melted chocolate or powdered sugar!

TOOLS & EQUIPMENT

mini muffin tin
mixing bowls
measuring cups
measuring spoons
silicone spatula
scoop

FLUFFY POTATO BAKE BITES

makes 12 muffins

INGREDIENTS

- 3 Yukon Gold potatoes
- 3 tablespoons unsalted butter
- ½ cup whole milk
- 4 tablespoons chopped green onions
- ½ cup grated Parmesan cheese
- 3 eggs
- 1 teaspoon salt
- ¼ teaspoon pepper

1. Preheat the oven to 400 degrees. Put paper liners in the muffin cups.
2. Peel and chop the potatoes. Fill a saucepan with water. Bring it to a boil. Add the potatoes. Cook 20 minutes. Drain the potatoes. Put them in a large mixing bowl.
3. Mash the potatoes with a fork until they are smooth.
4. Stir in the butter, milk, green onions, cheese, eggs, salt, and pepper.
5. Fill the paper liners halfway with batter. Bake 20 minutes. Let the muffins cool.

TOOLS & EQUIPMENT

paper liners
muffin tin
peeler
knife
cutting board
saucepan
strainer
large mixing bowl
fork
measuring cups
measuring spoons
scoop

MAC & CHEESY BITES

makes 12 muffins

INGREDIENTS

- non-stick cooking spray
- ¾ cup breadcrumbs
- 2 teaspoons olive oil
- 2 cups macaroni pasta
- 2 tablespoons unsalted butter
- 2 eggs
- 1 cup whole milk
- ½ cup grated Parmesan cheese
- 1 cup grated mozzarella cheese
- 1½ cups grated cheddar cheese

1. Preheat the oven to 350 degrees. Grease the muffin tin with non-stick cooking spray.
2. Put the breadcrumbs and oil in a small mixing bowl. Stir.
3. Fill a saucepan with water. Bring it to a boil. Add the macaroni pasta. Cook 8 minutes. Drain the pasta.
4. Put the pasta in a medium bowl. Add the butter and eggs. Stir to coat the pasta. Add the milk, Parmesan cheese, mozzarella cheese, and 1 cup of cheddar cheese. Stir.
5. Fill the muffin cups with the pasta mixture. Sprinkle the remaining cheddar cheese and breadcrumb mixture on top of the muffins. Bake 30 minutes or until light brown. Let the muffins cool.

TOOLS & EQUIPMENT

muffin tin
mixing bowls
measuring cups
measuring spoons
mixing spoon
saucepan
strainer
grater

CHEESY PIZZA PUFF PIECES

makes 24 muffins

INGREDIENTS

- non-stick cooking spray
- ¾ cup all-purpose flour
- ¾ teaspoon baking powder
- 1 teaspoon dried oregano
- ½ teaspoon salt
- ¾ cup whole milk
- 1 egg
- 1 cup chopped pepperoni
- 1½ cups grated mozzarella cheese
- ½ cup pizza sauce

1. Preheat the oven to 375 degrees. Grease the muffin tin with non-stick cooking spray.
2. Put the flour, baking powder, oregano, and salt in a large mixing bowl. Stir.
3. Whisk in the milk and egg. Stir in the pepperoni and mozzarella. Let the batter sit 10 minutes.
4. Divide the batter evenly between the muffin cups. Bake 20 minutes.
5. Put the pizza sauce in a small microwave-safe bowl. Heat it in the microwave. Serve it with the pizza puffs.

TOOLS & EQUIPMENT

mini muffin tin
measuring cups
measuring spoons
large mixing bowl
mixing spoon
whisk
knife
cutting board
grater
scoop
small microwave-safe bowl

HEARTY EGGS & BACON BRUNCH

makes 10 muffins

INGREDIENTS

- non-stick cooking spray
- 4 bacon strips
- 1 10-ounce (283-g) can biscuit dough
- ½ cup grated mozzarella cheese
- 3 eggs
- 2 tablespoons whole milk
- ½ teaspoon salt
- ½ teaspoon pepper
- ½ teaspoon oregano

1. Preheat the oven to 400 degrees. Line the baking sheet with foil. Grease the muffin tin with non-stick cooking spray.
2. Lay the bacon strips flat on the baking sheet. Bake 15 minutes or until golden brown. Let the bacon cool. Chop the bacon into pieces.
3. Separate the biscuits. Push one into each muffin cup. Press the dough to the sides of the cups. Leave a small ridge around the edge of each cup. Divide the cheese evenly between muffin cups.
4. In a medium mixing bowl, whisk together the eggs, milk, salt, pepper, and oregano. Fill each muffin cup halfway with the egg mixture. Sprinkle the bacon on top of the muffins.
5. Bake 12 minutes or until light brown. Serve the muffins while they're still warm.

TOOLS & EQUIPMENT

baking sheet
aluminum foil
muffin tin
knife
cutting board
grater
medium mixing bowl
measuring cups
measuring spoons
whisk

BANANA BREAD

makes 1 loaf

INGREDIENTS

- 1¾ cups sifted flour
- 1 tablespoon baking powder
- ½ teaspoon salt
- ⅓ cup butter
- ⅔ cup sugar
- 2 eggs
- 1 pound (0.45 kg) or 3 to 4 really ripe bananas

TOOLS & EQUIPMENT

- loaf pan
- sifter
- mixing bowls
- measuring cups
- measuring spoons
- whisk
- electric mixer
- mixing spoon
- knife
- cooling rack

1. Preheat the oven to 350 degrees. Grease a loaf pan and set it aside.
2. Whisk together the flour, baking powder, and salt in a mixing bowl.
3. In another mixing bowl, cream the butter until it is light and fluffy.
4. Add the sugar and the eggs to the butter and beat for another minute.
5. Add the peeled bananas to the egg mixture. Beat just until they are mixed in.
6. Stir in the flour mixture. Stir just until mixed.
7. Pour the batter into the prepared loaf pan.
8. Bake for about 60 minutes. A knife inserted in the middle of the loaf should come out clean. Cool on a cooling rack for about 10 minutes. Then remove the loaf from the pan and let it cool completely.

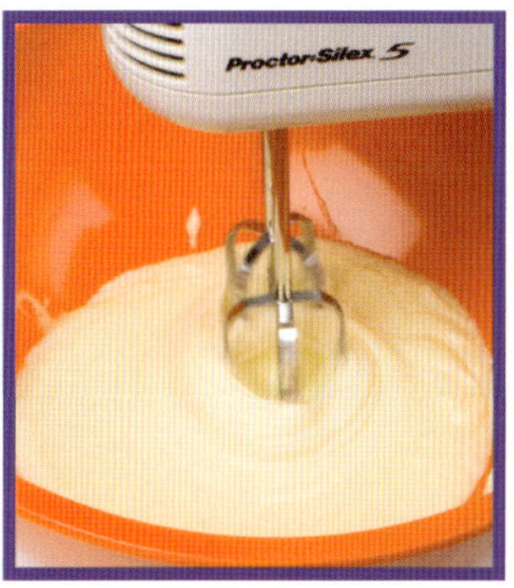

TRY THIS

Ripe bananas with black spots are perfect for making banana bread. If your bananas get ripe but you don't have time to bake, put them in the freezer. Allow the bananas to thaw before baking with them.

ZESTY ZUCCHINI BREAD

makes 2 loaves

INGREDIENTS

- 3 cups flour
- 1 teaspoon salt
- 1 teaspoon baking soda
- ¼ teaspoon baking powder
- 3 eggs
- 1 cup vegetable oil
- 1½ cups sugar
- 2 medium zucchini, shredded with a grater (about 2 cups)
- 1 tablespoon lemon zest
- 1 tablespoon vanilla extract
- 1 tablespoon cinnamon
- ¼ teaspoon nutmeg
- 1 cup chopped walnuts (optional)

1. Preheat the oven to 350 degrees. Grease and flour two loaf pans.
2. Whisk together the flour, salt, baking soda, and baking powder in a mixing bowl. Set this bowl aside.
3. In another mixing bowl, combine the eggs, vegetable oil, sugar, zucchini, lemon zest, vanilla, cinnamon, and nutmeg. Stir just until mixed.
4. Stir in the flour mixture. Add the walnuts, if you are using them.
5. Pour the mixture into the prepared loaf pans.
6. Bake for about 60 minutes. A toothpick inserted in the middle of a loaf should come out clean.
7. Cool the bread on a cooling rack for about 5 minutes. Then remove the loaves from the pans and set them on the rack. Let them cool completely.

TOOLS & EQUIPMENT

2 loaf pans
mixing bowls
measuring cups
measuring spoons
whisk
grater
zester
mixing spoon
silicone spatula
toothpick
cooling rack

COUNTRY PUMPKIN BREAD

makes 2 loaves

INGREDIENTS

- 2⅔ cups flour
- 2 teaspoons baking soda
- 1½ teaspoons salt
- 1 15-ounce (425-g) can pumpkin (not pumpkin pie filling)
- 3 cups sugar
- 4 eggs
- 1 cup vegetable oil
- ⅔ cup water
- 2 teaspoons nutmeg
- 2 teaspoons cinnamon
- 1½ teaspoons ground cloves
- 1 teaspoon allspice
- 1 cup chopped walnuts (optional)

TOOLS & EQUIPMENT

- mixing bowls
- measuring cups
- measuring spoons
- whisk
- mixing spoon
- silicone spatula
- 2 loaf pans
- toothpick
- cooling rack

1. Preheat the oven to 325 degrees.
2. Whisk together the flour, baking soda, and salt in a mixing bowl. Set this bowl aside.
3. In another mixing bowl, combine the pumpkin, sugar, eggs, vegetable oil, water, nutmeg, cinnamon, ground cloves, and allspice. Stir just until the ingredients are mixed.
4. Stir in the flour mixture. Add the walnuts, if you are using them.
5. Pour the mixture into ungreased loaf pans.
6. Bake for about 90 minutes. A toothpick inserted in the middle of a loaf should come out clean.
7. Cool the bread on a cooling rack for about 15 minutes. Then remove the loaves from the pans and set them on the rack. Let them cool completely.

SWEET POTATO BREAD

makes 1 loaf

INGREDIENTS

- 1 sweet potato
- 4 cups water
- non-stick cooking spray
- ¾ cup brown sugar
- ¾ cup sugar
- ½ cup butter
- 2 eggs
- ⅓ cup applesauce
- 1¾ cups all-purpose flour
- 1 teaspoon baking soda
- ½ teaspoon salt
- ½ teaspoon ground cinnamon
- ½ teaspoon ground nutmeg
- ½ cup chopped pecans

1. Peel the sweet potato. Cut it into ½-inch (1.3-cm) cubes. Boil the water in a saucepan. Add the sweet potato cubes. Cook 12 minutes. Drain the potatoes and place them in a mixing bowl. Mash the potatoes with a fork.
2. Preheat the oven to 350 degrees. Grease the bread pan with non-stick cooking spray.
3. In a small mixing bowl, cream the sugars and butter. Whisk in the eggs and applesauce.
4. In a large mixing bowl, combine the flour, baking soda, salt, cinnamon, and nutmeg. Add the sugar mixture to the flour mixture. Stir well.
5. Stir in the mashed sweet potatoes and nuts.
6. Pour the batter into the bread pan. Bake 60 minutes. Remove the pan from the oven. Let it cool.

TOOLS & EQUIPMENT

peeler
knife
cutting board
measuring cups
saucepan
strainer
mixing bowls
fork
bread pan
electric mixer
whisk
measuring spoons
silicone spatula

MARVELOUS MONKEY BREAD

makes about 15 servings

INGREDIENTS

3 7.5-ounce (213-g) cans refrigerated biscuits
2 tablespoons cinnamon
½ cup sugar
½ cup pecans or walnuts
½ cup raisins
6 tablespoons butter
¾ cup packed brown sugar

TOOLS & EQUIPMENT

tube pan or Bundt pan
kitchen scissors
measuring cups
measuring spoons
plastic bag
small saucepan
silicone spatula
cooling rack
plate

1. Preheat the oven to 350 degrees. Grease a tube pan or a Bundt pan.
2. Separate the biscuits. Cut each one in half with clean kitchen scissors. Mix the cinnamon and the sugar in a medium-sized plastic bag. Put about 10 biscuit pieces in the bag. Shake the bag until they are coated. Put the coated biscuit pieces in the bottom of the tube pan or Bundt pan.
3. When the bottom of the pan is covered, sprinkle on some of the raisins and nuts. Coat more biscuit pieces and arrange them in another layer. Sprinkle on more raisins and nuts. Continue layering biscuit pieces with raisins and nuts until there are no pieces left.
4. Put the butter and the brown sugar in a small saucepan and heat on medium high. Bring the mixture to a boil. Ask an adult helper to pour the hot mixture over the layered biscuits.
5. Bake for 35 minutes. Cool on a cooling rack for about 10 minutes.
6. Turn the pan over on a plate. Tap the bottom to loosen the monkey bread from the pan. Serve the bread while it's still warm.

MOLASSES BREAD IN A CAN

makes 2 loaves

INGREDIENTS

- butter
- ½ cup all-purpose flour
- ½ cup rye flour
- ½ cup cornmeal
- 1 teaspoon baking soda
- ½ teaspoon salt
- ½ teaspoon allspice
- 1 cup milk
- 1 teaspoon vanilla extract
- ½ cup molasses
- 5 cups water

1. Preheat the oven to 325 degrees. Grease the inside of each coffee can with butter.
2. Mix the flour, rye flour, cornmeal, baking soda, salt, and allspice in a large mixing bowl.
3. In a small bowl, mix together the milk and vanilla extract. Whisk the molasses into the milk mixture. Add the milk mixture to the flour mixture. Stir well.
4. Divide the batter evenly between the two cans. They should be about one-third full. Cover the tops of the cans with aluminum foil.
5. Tie string around the foil to hold it in place. Put the cans in the baking dish.
6. Ask an adult for help. Boil the water in a saucepan. Pour the boiling water in the baking dish. Bake 2 hours. Stick a skewer through the foil into the bread. If the skewer comes out clean the bread is done.
7. Let the bread cool in the can.

TOOLS & EQUIPMENT

2 6 × 4-inch (15 × 10-cm) coffee cans
measuring cups
measuring spoons
mixing bowls
mixing spoons
whisk
aluminum foil
string
8 × 8-inch baking dish
saucepan
wooden skewer

FRUITY FLAVORFUL BREAD

makes 12 servings

INGREDIENTS

non-stick cooking spray
2 cups all-purpose flour
1½ teaspoons pumpkin pie spice
1 teaspoon baking soda
½ teaspoon salt
1 teaspoon baking powder
1 cup bananas, mashed
1 6-ounce (170-g) can orange juice concentrate, thawed
2 eggs
1 cup raisins
½ teaspoon lemon extract

1. Preheat the oven to 350 degrees. Grease the loaf pan with non-stick cooking spray. Set it aside.
2. Put the flour, pumpkin pie spice, baking soda, salt, and baking powder in a large bowl. Stir with the mixing spoon.
3. Add the bananas, orange juice, eggs, raisins, and lemon extract. Stir well.
4. Pour the batter into the loaf pan. Make sure it is spread evenly.
5. Bake for 40 minutes, or until the loaf turns brown.
6. Remove the loaf from the oven. Let it cool for 10 minutes. Take the loaf out of the pan. Cut it into slices to share!

TOOLS & EQUIPMENT

9 × 5-inch loaf pan
measuring cups
measuring spoons
large mixing bowl
mixing spoon
silicone spatula
knife
cutting board

COOL CORNBREAD

makes one 8-inch (20-cm) square, about 9 pieces

INGREDIENTS

1 cup stone-ground cornmeal
1 cup flour
2 teaspoons baking powder
½ teaspoon salt
2 eggs
1 cup milk
¼ cup vegetable oil
2 tablespoons honey

1. Preheat the oven to 425 degrees. Grease the pan.
2. Whisk together the cornmeal, flour, baking powder, and salt in a mixing bowl.
3. In another mixing bowl, whisk together the eggs, milk, vegetable oil, and honey. Working quickly, stir the flour mixture into the egg mixture.
4. Pour the batter into the greased pan.
5. Bake for about 25 minutes. The top should be golden brown and the edges should pull away from the pan.
6. Cool on a cooling rack for about 5 minutes, then turn the pan over on the rack to remove the cornbread from the pan. Serve warm or at room temperature.

TOOLS & EQUIPMENT

8-inch square pan
mixing bowls
measuring cups
measuring spoons
whisk
mixing spoon
cooling rack

TRY THIS

Add 1 cup of fresh or frozen corn kernels to the batter when you stir in the flour mixture. Add ½ cup of grated cheddar cheese to the flour mixture. Dice 1 jalapeño pepper and add it to the egg mixture.

SAVORY HERB PULL-APARTS

makes about 15 servings

INGREDIENTS

- ¼ cup butter
- 1 clove garlic
- 3 7.5-ounce (213-g) cans refrigerated biscuits
- 1 tablespoon chopped fresh parsley
- 1 tablespoon chopped fresh oregano
- 1 tablespoon chopped fresh thyme
- 1 cup shredded Italian cheese mix (with Asiago, Parmesan, and Romano cheeses)

1. Preheat the oven to 350 degrees. Grease a tube pan or a Bundt pan.
2. Melt the butter in a small saucepan over medium heat. Use a garlic press to squeeze the garlic into the warm butter.
3. Separate the biscuits. Brush a third of the biscuits with garlic butter. Cover the bottom of the tube pan or Bundt pan with the buttered biscuits. Sprinkle a third of the herbs and a third of the cheese over the biscuits.
4. Butter half of the remaining biscuits and place them in the pan. Sprinkle herbs and cheese over the second layer. Brush the rest of the biscuits with garlic butter and put them in the pan. Top the biscuits with the remaining herbs and cheese.
5. Bake for about 35 minutes. The top of the bread should be golden brown. Cool on a cooling rack for about 10 minutes.
6. Turn the pan over on a plate. Tap the bottom to loosen the bread from the pan. Serve the bread while it is still warm.

TOOLS & EQUIPMENT

tube pan or Bundt Pan
small saucepan
garlic press
basting brush
measuring cups
measuring spoons
cooling rack
plate

YEASTED BREADS

Yeasted bread dough must be kneaded by hand or with an electric mixer. A dough is a mix of wet and dry ingredients that is thick enough to hold its shape. When you make bread with yeast, you let the dough rise. This can take an hour or more. Then you punch down the dough and let it rise again. This process takes hours. But the result is worth it!

Morning Muffin Biscuits

Sticky Cinnamon Rolls

Pepperoni Pizza Bread
Classic Sandwich Bread
Buttery
House Rolls

STICKY CINNAMON ROLLS

makes 12 rolls

INGREDIENTS

- ¾ cup milk
- ¾ cup butter
- non-stick cooking spray
- 3 cups all-purpose flour
- 2¼ teaspoon instant yeast
- 1¼ cup brown sugar
- ½ teaspoon salt
- 1 egg
- ¼ cup water
- 1¼ tablespoons ground cinnamon

1. Put the milk in a small microwave-safe bowl. Heat it in the microwave for 1 minute. Add ¼ cup butter. Stir until the butter is melted. Grease the baking dish with non-stick cooking spray.
2. In a large mixing bowl, mix together 3 cups flour, yeast, ¼ cup brown sugar, and salt. Stir in the milk mixture, egg, and water.
3. Sprinkle flour on a cutting board. Set the dough on the flour. Knead it until it's smooth. Put the dough in a bowl. Cover the bowl with a towel. Let it sit 10 minutes.
4. Mix 1 cup brown sugar, cinnamon, and ½ cup butter in a small bowl.
5. Roll out the dough into a 12 × 5-inch (30 × 13-cm) rectangle. Spread the brown sugar mixture over the dough.
6. Roll up the dough starting at a short edge.
7. Slice the roll into 12 pieces. Place the slices on their sides in the baking dish. Cover the dish and let it sit 30 minutes. Preheat the oven to 375 degrees. Bake 25 to 30 minutes. Remove the dish from the oven. Let the rolls cool.

TOOLS & EQUIPMENT

measuring cups
small microwave-safe bowl
8 × 8-inch baking dish
large mixing bowl
measuring spoons
silicone spatula
cutting board
clean kitchen towel
rolling pin
knife

BUTTERY HOUSE ROLLS

makes 36 rolls

INGREDIENTS

- 1 package active dry yeast
- ¼ cup warm water
- 1 cup whole milk
- 3 tablespoons sugar
- 1½ teaspoons salt
- ¾ cup butter
- 1 large egg
- 3½ cups all-purpose flour
- non-stick cooking spray

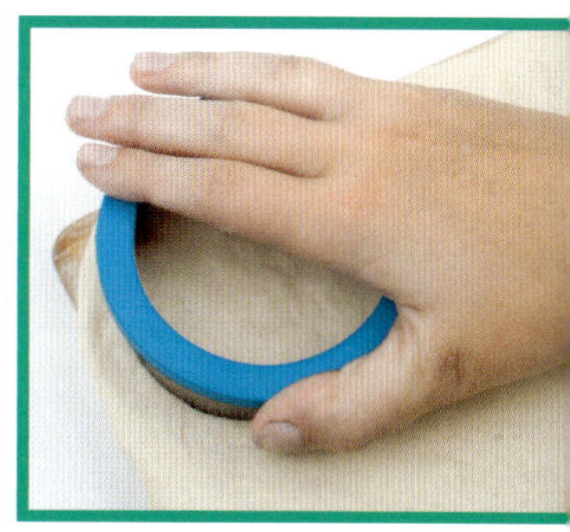

1. Whisk the yeast and warm water together. Let it sit for 5 minutes. Heat the milk in the microwave for 1 minute. Pour the milk into a large bowl. Stir in the sugar, salt, and ¼ cup butter. Whisk in the yeast mixture and egg.
2. Add the flour. Stir until the mixture becomes doughy. Sprinkle flour on a clean surface. Set the dough on the flour. Knead it for 4 or 5 minutes, until it is smooth. Put the dough in a bowl. Cover the bowl with plastic wrap. Let it sit 90 minutes.
3. Preheat the oven to 350 degrees. Grease the baking sheet with non-stick cooking spray and set it aside. Melt ½ cup butter in the microwave.
4. Uncover the dough. Punch the dough down.
5. Roll out the dough until it's ½ inch (1.3 cm) thick.
6. Use the cookie cutter to cut circles of dough. Dip them in the melted butter. Fold them in half and place them on the baking sheet. Cover the baking sheet with a towel. Let it sit 30 minutes. Remove the towel. Bake for 30 minutes.

TOOLS & EQUIPMENT

measuring cups
mixing bowls
whisk
measuring spoons
mixing spoon
plastic wrap
baking sheet
rolling pin
round cookie cutter
clean kitchen towel

CLASSIC SANDWICH BREAD

makes 3 loaves

INGREDIENTS

- 1½ tablespoons salt
- 1½ tablespoons active dry yeast
- 3 cups warm water
- 4½ cups all-purpose flour
- 2 cups semolina flour
- non-stick cooking spray

1. Put the salt, yeast, and warm water in a mixing bowl. Stir. Let it sit 10 minutes.
2. Add the all-purpose flour and semolina flour. Stir until a sticky dough forms, about 5 minutes.
3. Cover the bowl with a towel. Let it sit 2 hours. Lightly punch the dough down. Cover the bowl with plastic wrap. Chill the dough in the refrigerator overnight.
4. Preheat the oven to 450 degrees. Grease the bread pan with non-stick cooking spray and set it aside. Cover your hands with flour. Form one-third of the dough into a loaf shape.
5. Place the dough in the bread pan.
6. Make several shallow, diagonal cuts on the top of the loaf. Bake 35 minutes. Take it out of the oven and let it cool.
7. Repeat steps 4 through 6 to bake the remaining dough.

TOOLS & EQUIPMENT

measuring cups
measuring spoons
large mixing bowl
mixing spoon
clean kitchen towel
plastic wrap
bread pan
knife

SIMPLE ROSEMARY BREAD

makes 1 loaf

INGREDIENTS

- 2½ teaspoons active dry yeast
- 1 teaspoon sugar
- 14 tablespoons warm water
- 1 teaspoon garlic powder
- 2½ cups all-purpose flour
- butter
- 2 tablespoons olive oil
- 1 teaspoon salt
- 1 teaspoon dried oregano
- 2 teaspoons dried rosemary

1. Put the yeast, sugar, and 5 tablespoons of warm water in a small bowl. Let it sit for 10 minutes.
2. In a large bowl, stir together the yeast mixture, garlic powder, and flour. Add 9 tablespoons water, 1 tablespoon at a time, until the mixture becomes a sticky dough.
3. Sprinkle flour on a clean surface. Knead the dough on the flour for about 1 minute.
4. Grease a medium bowl and a baking sheet with butter. Place the dough in the bowl. Cover it with the towel. Let it sit 30 minutes.
5. Preheat the oven to 475 degrees. Knead the dough for 1 minute on a floured surface. Flatten the dough into a 9 × 5-inch (23 × 13-cm) rectangle. Place it on the baking sheet. Poke dents in the dough with the end of a mixing spoon.
6. Brush the dough with the olive oil. Sprinkle on salt, oregano, and rosemary. Bake 15 minutes. Take it out and let it cool.

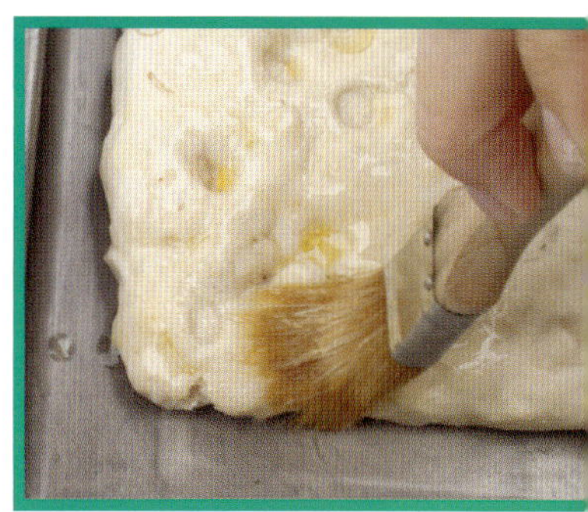

TOOLS & EQUIPMENT

measuring spoons
measuring cups
mixing bowls
mixing spoon
baking sheet
clean kitchen towel
basting brush

MORNING MUFFIN BISCUITS

makes 6 biscuits

INGREDIENTS

- 1 cup whole milk
- 1 tablespoon sugar
- 1 tablespoon butter
- 1 package instant yeast
- 2 cups and 1 tablespoon bread flour
- ¾ teaspoon salt
- 1 tablespoon cornmeal

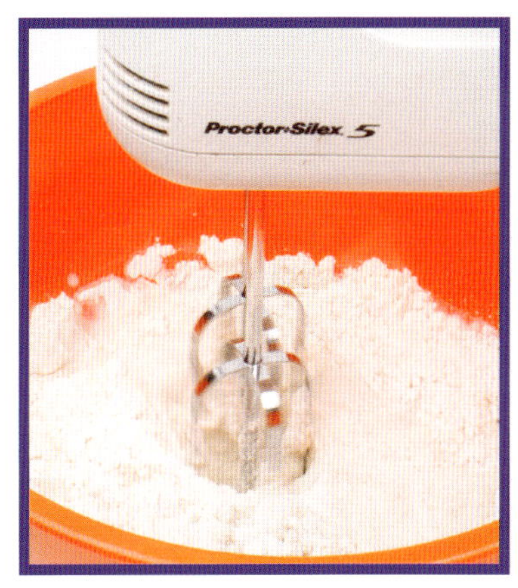

1. Put the milk in a microwave-safe bowl. Heat it in the microwave for 30 seconds. Stir in the sugar and butter. Let it cool.
2. Put the yeast, 2 cups flour, and salt in a mixing bowl. Add the milk mixture. Beat with an electric mixer until smooth. Cover the bowl with a towel. Let it sit 12 hours.
3. Stir the cornmeal and 1 tablespoon flour together in a bowl. Uncover the bowl of dough. Cut the dough into six equal pieces.
4. Heat the frying pan on medium heat. Scoop out a piece of dough with a spoon. Be careful not to deflate the dough. Coat the dough with the cornmeal mixture. Place it in the pan.
5. Cook the dough for 10 minutes. Flip it over with a spatula. Cook it for 10 more minutes.
6. Repeat steps 4 and 5 until all of the biscuits are cooked.

TOOLS & EQUIPMENT

measuring cups
microwave-safe bowl
mixing bowls
mixing spoons
measuring spoons
electric mixer
clean kitchen towel
knife
frying pan
spoon
spatula

PEPPERONI PIZZA BREAD

makes 1 loaf

INGREDIENTS

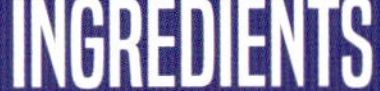

- non-stick cooking spray
- 1 egg
- 1 teaspoon garlic powder
- 1 tablespoon flour
- premade pizza dough
- 6 ounces (170 g) sliced pepperoni sausage
- 1½ cups shredded mozzarella cheese
- ¼ cup Parmesan cheese
- 1½ teaspoons Italian seasoning

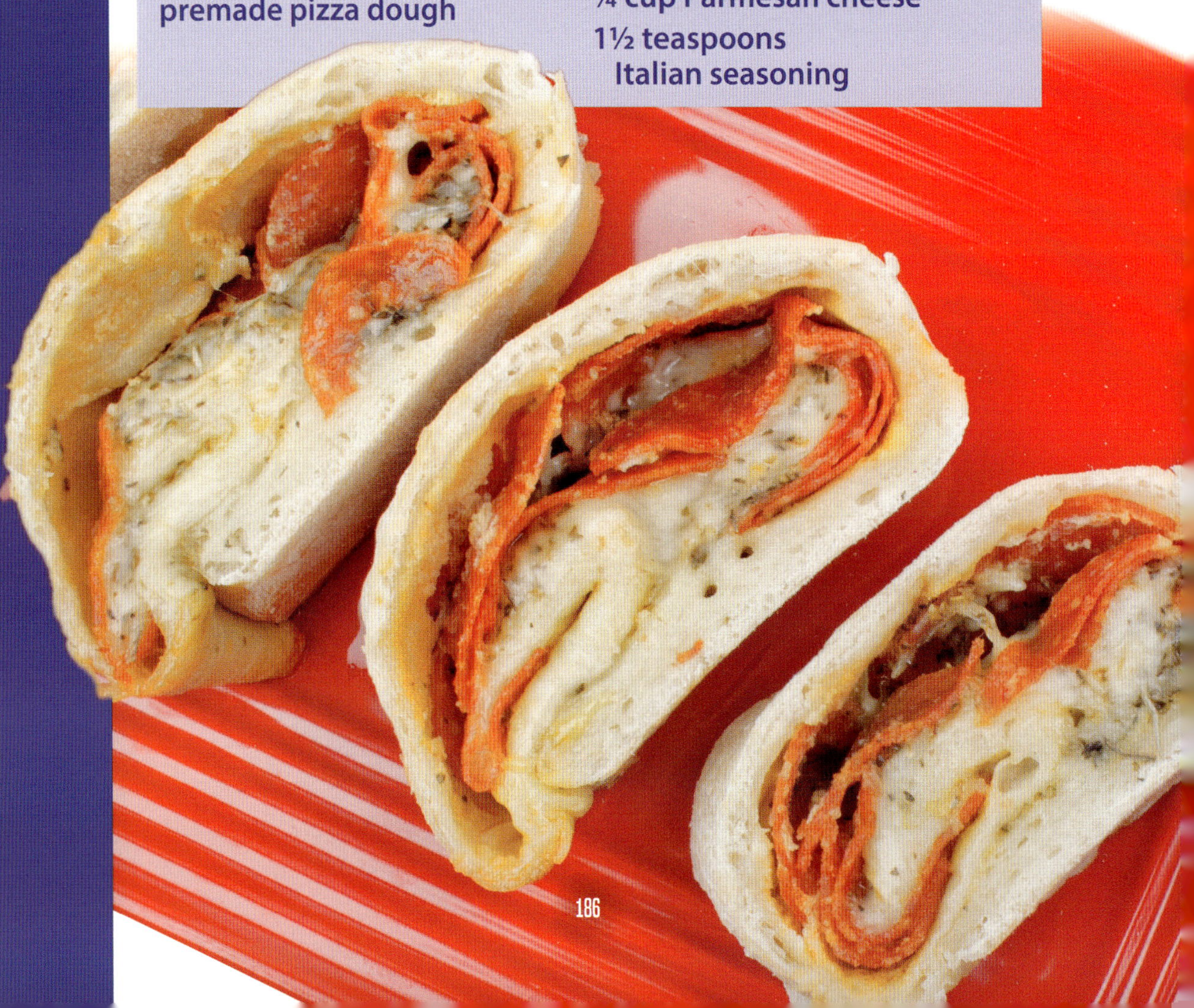

1. Preheat the oven to 375 degrees. Grease a baking sheet with non-stick cooking spray. Mix the egg and the garlic powder together in a small bowl.
2. Sprinkle the flour on the cutting board. Set the pizza dough on the cutting board. Roll the dough into a 12 × 9-inch (30 × 23-cm) rectangle. Brush the dough with the egg mixture.
3. Arrange the pepperoni, mozzarella cheese, and Parmesan cheese on the dough. Sprinkle on the Italian seasoning.
4. Starting at one long edge, roll up the dough. Pinch the ends closed.
5. Put the dough on the baking sheet with the seam facing down. Bake 40 minutes. Take the roll out of the oven. Cut it into slices.

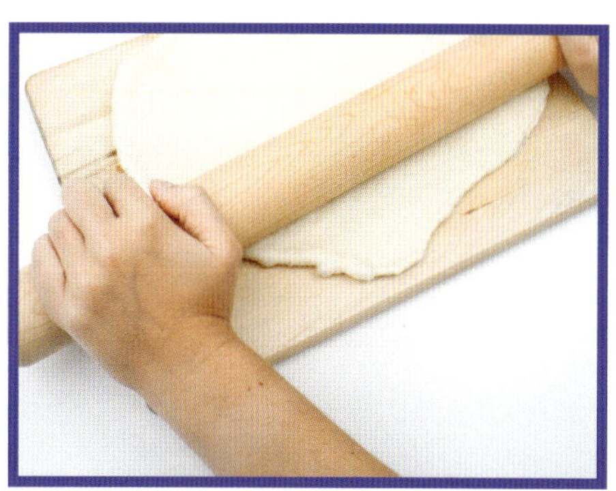

TOOLS & EQUIPMENT

baking sheet
measuring spoons
mixing bowl
mixing spoon
cutting board
rolling pin
basting brush
measuring cups
knife

GLOSSARY

bacteria
tiny, one-celled organisms that can only be seen through a microscope.

crimp
to pinch or press something to make it bent or wavy.

dollop
a spoonful of something, usually a topping such as jam or whipped cream.

drizzle
to pour in a thin stream.

enhance
to increase or improve.

extract
a product made by concentrating the juices taken from something such as a plant.

formula
a combination of specific amounts of different ingredients or elements.

germ
a tiny, living organism that can make people sick.

insert
to put something into something else.

knead
to press, fold, and stretch something, such as dough.

kuchen
German for "cake."

leavening
a substance such as yeast or baking soda that makes baked goods rise.

pasteurized
something, such as milk or eggs, that has been heated to a certain temperature for a specific amount of time in order to kill harmful germs.

protein
a substance needed for good health, found naturally in meat, eggs, beans, nuts, and milk.

savory
tasty and flavorful but not sweet.

simmer
to cook something so it bubbles gently.

tapioca
a food made from the starchy root of the tropical cassava plant.

TO LEARN MORE

FURTHER READINGS

The Best Ever Cake Book. DK Publishing, 2022.

The Big, Fun Kids Baking Book. Hearst Home Kids, 2021.

Goldman, Duff. *Super Good Cookies for Kids*. HarperCollins, 2022.

ONLINE RESOURCES

To learn more about baking, please visit **abdobooklinks.com** or scan this QR code. These links are routinely monitored and updated to provide the most current information available.

INDEX

allergies, 8

bars, 76, 94–97
biscuits, 154–155, 164–165, 172–173, 184–185

cake, 6, 18, 20, 22, 24, 26–43, 76
cake mix, 28, 44–53, 56–57, 64–67, 70–75
caramel, 94–95
cheese, 148–155, 171–173, 186–187
chocolate, 11, 16, 19, 28–29, 32–33, 40–41, 46–49, 54–55, 58–61, 64–67, 74–75, 78–79, 84–85, 88–89, 92–97, 108–109, 134–135, 140–143, 147
citrus zest, 11, 23, 26–27, 62–63, 90–91, 137, 158–159
conversion charts, 9
cookies, 23, 74–75, 76, 78–91
cornmeal, 166–167, 170–171, 184–185
cream, 13
cream cheese, 46–47, 52–53, 60–63, 86–87, 138–139
cream of tartar, 88–89
cupcakes, 18, 24, 44–75

doneness, 22, 27, 39, 93, 107, 157, 159, 161, 167
double boilers, 19, 32–33, 108–109, 117

electric mixers, 21, 26–31, 34–35, 42–43, 45–47, 49, 51, 53, 60–61, 63, 67, 69, 71, 78–81, 83, 85, 89–91, 108–109, 156–157, 163, 174, 185

extracts, 12, 26–29, 32–33, 40–55, 58–63, 66–71, 74–75, 78–93, 106–111, 122–147, 158–159, 166–169

food coloring, 46–47, 50–51, 56–57, 70–71
frosting, 6, 18, 20, 40–41, 44–53, 62–63, 66–75
fruit, 11, 13, 15, 23, 26–29, 32–35, 38–39, 42–43, 62–63, 66–67, 80–81, 86–87, 98, 104–105, 110–113, 116–119, 122–127, 130–131, 136–139, 142–143, 146–147, 156–157, 160–161, 164–165, 168–169

gelatin, 50–51
ginger, 118–119, 146–147
granola, 130–131

herbs, 66–67, 152–155, 172–173, 182–183
honey, 14, 36–37, 170–171

ice cream, 26–27, 64–65, 104–107

juice, 15, 36–37, 50–51, 105, 110–111, 116–117, 124–125, 137, 144–145, 168–169

lemon curd, 62–63, 117

meat, 114–115, 152–155, 186–187
muffins, 120, 122–155

nuts, 7–8, 12, 14, 30–31, 36–37, 60–61, 68–69, 78–79, 82–83, 88–89, 94–95, 106–107, 124–125, 128–129, 141, 158–165

oats, 80–81, 96–97, 124–127

peaks, 23, 35, 89
peanut butter, 68–69, 79, 141
pies, 15–16, 98, 100–115
potatoes, 114–115, 148–149, 162–163
pudding mix, 50–51, 64–67, 72–73

quick breads, 120, 156–173

rolls, 176–179

safety, 6–8, 12
seeds, 10, 12, 136–137
spices, 36–41, 52–53, 60–61, 79–81, 90–93, 96–97, 104–105, 112–115, 118–119, 124–133, 142–149, 154–155, 158–169, 176–177, 186–187
sprinkles, 44–45, 48–49, 58–59
syrup, 14, 36–37, 90, 96–97, 106–107, 140–141

tarts, 98, 100–103, 116–119

vegetables, 13, 52–53, 114–115, 124–125, 128–129, 158–159, 171

whipped cream, 24, 29, 34–35, 54–57, 108–109

yeast, 120, 174, 176–185
yeasted breads, 174, 176–185
yogurt, 134–135, 140–141

PHOTO CREDITS

Cover Photographs: Mighty Media, Inc.
Interior Photographs: Adobe Stock, p. 13 (left); Andrjuss/Shutterstock Images, p. 125 (bottom); GrigoryL/Shutterstock Images, p. 10 (left); igor kisselev/Shutterstock Images, p. 16 (bottom); Jaroslaw Grudzinski/Shutterstock Images, p. 129 (bottom); mates/Adobe Stock, p. 29 (bottom); Mighty Media, Inc., pp. 1, 2 (left), 3, 4, 5, 9, 10 (right top, right middle), 12, 13 (right bottom), 14 (top, middle), 15, 16 (top), 17, 18, 19, 20, 21, 22, 23, 24-25, 26, 27, 28, 29 (top left, top middle, top right), 30, 31, 32, 33, 34, 35, 36, 37, 38, 39, 40, 41, 42, 43, 44, 45 (top left, top right), 47, 48, 49, 50, 51, 52, 53, 54, 55, 56, 57, 58, 59, 60, 61, 62, 63, 64, 65, 66, 67, 68, 69, 70, 71, 72, 73 (top left, top right), 74, 75, 76-77, 78, 79, 80, 81, 82, 83, 84, 85, 86, 87, 88, 89, 90, 91, 92, 93, 94, 95, 96, 97, 98, 99, 100, 101, 102, 103, 104, 105, 106, 107, 108, 109, 110, 111, 112, 113, 114, 115, 116, 117, 118, 119, 120, 121, 122, 123, 124, 125 (top, middle), 126, 127 (top, middle), 128, 129 (top left, top right), 130, 131, 132, 133, 134, 135, 136, 137, 138, 139, 140, 141, 142, 143 (top left, top right), 144, 145, 146, 147, 148, 149 (top, middle), 150, 151, 152, 153, 154, 155, 156, 157, 158, 159, 160, 161, 162, 163, 164, 165, 166, 167, 168, 169, 170, 171, 172, 173, 174-175, 176, 177, 178, 179, 180, 181, 182-183, 184-185, 186, 187 (right top, right middle, right bottom); mphillips007/iStockphoto, p. 187 (left); O.Bellini/Shutterstock Images, p. 73 (bottom); Phant/Shutterstock Images, p. 13 (right middle); Potapovpaladin/Shutterstock Images, p. 11 (top), 46; Sailorr/Shutterstock Images, p. 143 (bottom); Shutterstock Images, pp. 2 (right), 10 (right bottom), 13 (right top), 14 (bottom), 45 (bottom), 127 (bottom); StefanoT/Shutterstock Images, p. 11 (bottom); William E. Fehr/Shutterstock Images, 149 (bottom)

Design Elements: Mighty Media, Inc.